A gift for:

_____

Listen to advice and accept instruction,
and in the end you will be wise.

Proverbs 19:20

From:

_____

The Best Advice I Ever Got
Copyright © 2007 by Zondervan
ISBN 978-0-310-81454-2

Internet addresses (websites, blogs, etc.) and telephone numbers printed
in this book are offered as a resource to you. These are not intended in
any way to be or imply an endorsement on the part of Zondervan, nor do we
vouch for the content of these sites and numbers for the life of this book.

Requests for information should be addressed to:
Inspirio, the gift group of Zondervan
Grand Rapids, Michigan 49530
www.inspiriogifts.com

Compiler: SnapdragonGroup℠ Editorial Services
Project Manager: Kim Zeilstra
Design Manager: Michael J. Williams
Production Manager: Matt Nolan
Design: The Design Works Group
Cover image: Getty Images/Photodisc/Steve Cole

A special thanks to Daniel Decker and Melanie VanBurch for their help in
the production of this book.

Printed in China
07 08 09/4 3 2 1

THE BEST ADVICE I EVER GOT

Wit and Wisdom for Graduates

inspirio®

To accept good advice
is but to increase
one's own ability.

Johann Wolfgang von Goethe

Think for a moment how great it would be if you could simply sail through your life, avoiding pitfalls, making good choices, identifying and steering clear of danger. But life is filled with unknowns. Where can you possibly gain the tools you need to ensure a successful journey?

The Best Advice I Ever Got is an excellent source of advice from people in every walk of life — in business, ministry, entertainment, sports, and publishing. These high achievers have passed along the very best advice they've received—advice that has helped them become the best and brightest in their fields and winners in their personal lives. They've told us how the advice came to them and how it changed their thinking and motivated them to transform obstacles into opportunities. We've added scriptures so you can see for yourself that their advice lines up with God's Word.

As you leave one phase of your life and enter the next, take this book along. Read it often and consider the significance of each lesson. Then share it with others.

Table of Contents

The best advice I ever got ...

Truth and time
walk hand in hand.

I received this counsel from Dr. George Sweeting, former president of the Moody Bible Institute, while hoping to get him to commiserate over unkind things said about me. He went on, "With visibility comes scrutiny. Learn from valid criticism, but as for the other, remember that truth and time walk hand in hand."

Little did I know then that more unsought visibility — and thus more scrutiny — was in my future and that Dr. Sweeting's wise counsel would make it bearable. Allowing the passage of time to reveal the truth has freed me from the compulsion to defend myself. It has enabled me to stay focused on the task at hand.

Jerry B. Jenkins

Bestselling Author

Vindicate me, O Lord, for I have walked in my integrity;
... Examine me, O Lord, and prove me; test my heart
and my mind. For Your loving-kindness is before my
eyes, and I have walked in Your truth [faithfully].

Psalm 26:1–3 AMP

The Lord will vindicate his people
and have compassion on his servants.

Psalm 135:14

He whose walk is blameless
and who does what is righteous,
who speaks the truth from his heart ...
He who does these things
will never be shaken.

Psalm 15:2, 5

Jerry B. Jenkins is the former vice president of publishing and currently a member of the board of trustees for the **Moody Bible Institute of Chicago**. He is also the author of more than 160 books, including the *Left Behind* series which has sold more than 63 million copies.

The former editor of *Moody Magazine*, Jenkins' writing has appeared in *Time*, *Reader's Digest*, *Parade*, *Guideposts*, and dozens of Christian periodicals. In a May 24, 2004, cover story, he and Tim LaHaye were profiled in *Newsweek* magazine. The writer of several nonfiction books, Jerry had the privilege of assisting Dr. Billy Graham with his memoirs, *Just As I Am*, also a *New York Times* bestseller.

Jerry owns Jenkins Entertainment, a filmmaking company in Los Angeles, as well as the Christian Writers Guild, which aims to train tomorrow's professional Christian writers and has nearly 2,000 members worldwide.

The best advice I ever got . . .

Follow your dreams,
but remember —
nothing is a substitute
for hard work.

My dad instilled in me that success is loving what you do for a living, because so much of life is spent doing it. But he also believed in a strong work ethic. My first dream was to play major league baseball, and my father supported my dream until my career ended in injury. Then, with little experience but a lot of hard work, I began my second dream of becoming a successful entertainer in show business.

I've spent the last thirty years singing, doing impressions, and making audiences laugh. God opened doors for me, but I made sure that I was ready when each one opened.

Danny Gans

Entertainer Extraordinaire

The plans of the diligent lead to profit.
Proverbs 21:5

The desires of the diligent are fully satisfied.
Proverbs 13:4

Whatever your hand finds to do, do it with all your might.
Ecclesiastes 9:10

Whatever you do, work at it with all your heart, as working
for the Lord, not for men, since you know that you will
receive an inheritance from the Lord as a reward.
Colossians 3:23–24

Gans' boyhood dream was to play third base for the Los Angeles Dodgers. Drafted by the Kansas City Royals after high school and the Chicago White Sox after college, this All-American did go on to the minor leagues. Not long after, however, his world was turned upsidedown by a career-ending injury.

Blessed with a marvelous singing voice and the ability to make people laugh, Gans was encouraged to shift his focus to entertainment—and a new career was born.

Gans spent the next fifteen years honing his skills, often playing to stadium-sized crowds for Fortune 500 companies. However, Danny found himself longing to be home with his wife and three children. When he was presented with the opportunity to move his show to Las Vegas where he could settle down, he took it, and for the last six years, he has performed consistently sold-out shows in his 1,265-seat theater at the Mirage. Danny also has held the position of Entertainer of the Year in Las Vegas for nine consecutive years.

The best advice I ever got ...

The need is not the call.

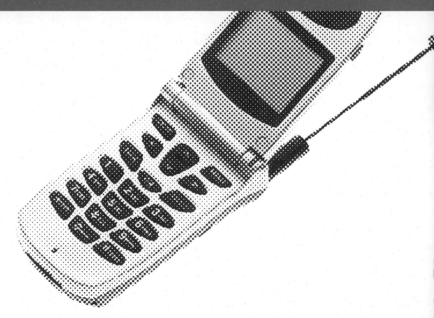

I received this advice many years ago in a message from retired minister **T. K. Shoemaker**. I was a young Christian at the time, starting my life in ministry and answering *yes!* to almost every urging to fill a needed position. *After all,* I thought, *if they asked me to do it, they must think I can do it. So this must be God telling me to do it.* Within two years, I burned out like a fuse on a firecracker with no explosive powder. I thought I was being a good servant, a hard worker in God's kingdom. Confused, I wondered, *What went wrong?*

Many people spend a majority of their lives in professions from which they receive little or no emotional fulfillment. They followed the advice of friends, family, or employment recruiters who told of specific job opportunities with immediate "need to fill" positions. God has blessed each of us with unique gifts and calls us into specific areas of service or employment. Don't settle for less than God's best for you. Seek the position where your talents will best glorify God and fulfill his unique call on your life.

Sharon Burton

President and Co-Founder of Overcomers Recovery Support

God has placed each part in the body just as he wanted it to be. If all the parts were the same, how could there be a body? As it is, there are many parts. But there is only one body.

1 Corinthians 12:18–20 NIrV

We are God's [own] handiwork (His workmanship), recreated in Christ Jesus, [born anew] that we may do those good works which God predestined (planned beforehand) for us [taking paths which He prepared ahead of time], that we should walk in them [living the good life which He prearranged and made ready for us to live].

Ephesians 2:10 AMP

It was [God] who gave some to be apostles, some to be prophets, some to be evangelists, and some to be pastors and teachers, to prepare God's people for works of service, so that the body of Christ may be built up until we all reach unity in the faith and in the knowledge of the Son of God and become mature, attaining to the whole measure of the fullness of Christ.

Ephesians 4:11–13

Sharon Burton is the president and co-founder of Overcomers Recovery Support, a biblically based twelve-step program, widely recognized as an effective tool for churches, treatment centers, and prisons to provide a practical, spiritual plan of recovery for people who struggle with addictions and other life-controlling issues.

Ordained to the ministry in 1987, Sharon traveled to prisons throughout the United States, served on the board of directors for the Coalition of Prison Evangelists, and co-authored the recovery curriculum *A Daily Choice, Overcoming Life-Controlling Problems.* From 1993 to 1995, Sharon and her husband, Charles, served as missionaries in the former communist country of Estonia, where they trained prison chaplains, established the first Christian ministry in the history of the prison system, and taught Christian volunteers how to mentor recovering alcoholics. Today the Overcomers program has expanded to Russia, Scotland, Ireland, England, Holland, and Canada.

The best advice I ever got ...

1. **Never lose the ability to say, "Thank you."**

2. **Keep a solid reputation.**

3. **Protect your signature.**

When I was first starting out in show business, I met Groucho Marx in the Beverly Hills Polo Lounge. I asked him if he had any advice he could give me, and he replied that these were the three most important things to remember.

Your talent can never be destroyed or taken away from you; but sign the wrong contract or not be true to your word, and you will be out of the industry quicker than you can say, "Groucho."

From the first agreements I entered with Columbia Records and CBS to all the ones since, I have remembered the advice that Groucho shared with me about making honorable deals. I believe God used his words of wisdom as the catalysts that have enabled me to enjoy forty-five years in show business.

Thank you, Groucho!

Tony Orlando
Award-Winning Entertainer

A good name is more desirable than great riches;
to be esteemed is better than silver or gold.
Proverbs 22:1

Do not let anyone lead you astray.
He who does what is right is righteous,
just as [God] is righteous.
1 John 3:7

Lord, who may dwell in your sanctuary?
Who may live on your holy mountain?
Those whose walk is blameless,
who do what is righteous,
who speak the truth from their hearts;
who have no slander on their tongues,
who do their neighbors no wrong,
who cast no slur on others; . . .
who keep their oaths even when it hurts.
Psalm 15:1–4 TNIV

One of America's most enduring stars, **Tony** recently celebrated the thirty-third anniversary of his recording "Tie a Yellow Ribbon 'Round the Ole Oak Tree," which has become an American anthem of hope and homecoming for POWs, hostages, and war veterans. From million-selling recordings (including five number-one hits), a popular television variety series, movies, and Broadway, he has conquered every facet of show business.

Orlando remains one of America's best-loved personalities. He has been a recipient of the People's Choice Award, three American Music Awards, and in 1990 was awarded a star on the Hollywood Walk of Fame. He currently lives in Branson, Missouri, where he has performed more than 2,000 shows and has been named Branson's Entertainer and Vocalist of the Year.

The best advice I ever got ...

You ought to write a book!

My mentor — author and speaker, Florence Littauer — gave me this advice in 1978. I told her that I didn't know how to write, only had a high-school education, and couldn't spell very well. But she saw something in me and encouraged me to step out and try something new.

I have now written seventy-four books, with more on the way. I never imagined that one day there would be more than five-million copies of my books in print.

You may not be called to write a book, but you should step out and try your hand at whatever God has placed in your heart. If you are doing what he has called you to do, you will be successful — regardless of the obstacles you might see in the road ahead.

Emilie Barnes

Renowned Author and Speaker

A gift opens the way for the giver
and ushers him into the presence of the great.
Proverbs 18:16

I have filled [you] with the Spirit of God, with skill,
ability and knowledge in all kinds of crafts.
Exodus 31:3

The LORD God is a sun and shield;
the LORD bestows favor and honor;
no good thing does he withhold
from those whose walk is blameless.
Psalm 84:11

Each one should use whatever gift he has received to serve others,
faithfully administering God's grace in its various forms. If anyone
speaks, he should do it as one speaking the very words of God. If
anyone serves, he should do it with the strength God provides, so
that in all things God may be praised through Jesus Christ.
1 Peter 4:10–11

Emilie and her husband, Bob, have partnered in More Hours in My Day Ministries for more than thirty years. In addition to teaching women creative ways to get organized, Emilie has shared her personal journey through life-threatening cancer, recovery, and beyond for the last eight years. Together, she and Bob have written sixty-five books.

Emilie is listed in *100 Christian Women Who Changed the 20th Century* (Revell). She is an enthusiastic media guest who has shared practical insights and personal experiences on hundreds of radio and television programs, such as *The 700 Club*, *Focus on the Family*, *Family Life*, Trinity Broadcasting Network, and Moody Broadcasting Network.

The best advice I ever got ...

Highly esteem, reverence, and cherish God's Word, the Bible.

From early childhood, I received this training from my parents, and it became an integral part of my life. The Bible was treated with utmost respect in our home. We never placed another book or object on top of it, and we read it three times a day — every meal and sometimes again in the evening. My parents lived their lives according to its precepts and raised my four siblings and me to do the same. God's Word has given me a biblical, Christian worldview. It requires self-discipline to develop the habit of looking at everything from a scriptural viewpoint, but the result is a blessed and fruitful life.

For several years, I worked for the Youth Action Coalition, preparing and coaching young people to debate, lobby, or speak at public hearings where moral issues — such as abortion, homosexuality, pornography, or rock-music lyrics — were on the agenda. The Bible was the standard by which all things were measured, and it gave all of us confidence in our beliefs because they were verified by Scripture. His Word is an anchor in uncertain times, a light in the darkness, and the hope for our souls.

Annetta Small

Counselor and Conservative Activist

I have kept my feet from every evil path
so that I might obey your word.
I have not departed from your laws,
for you yourself have taught me.
How sweet are your words to my taste,
sweeter than honey to my mouth!
I gain understanding from your precepts;
therefore I hate every wrong path.
Your word is a lamp to my feet
and a light for my path.

Psalm 119:101–105

Jesus replied, "Blessed rather are
those who hear the word of God and obey it."

Luke 11:28

Pastor's wife **Annetta Small** has always been active in church life, including running a Christian school for three years. In the past, the Smalls have been heavily involved in conservative Christian politics in Washington State, and Annetta has made numerous appearances on both local and national radio programs. From 1991–1997, she organized and advised the Youth Action Coalition (YAC), where she trained young people for effective Christian political involvement, grooming members to appear on both radio and television to debate ACLU attorneys and to discuss current issues from a biblical point of view.

From 1997–2002, Annetta served as the West Coast director for Kerusso Ministries. Annetta's present ministry focuses on the discipleship of girls and women, especially those who have recently begun their walk with Christ.

The best advice I ever got ...

Read the Bible.

Most of my life I had all the things the world says will make you happy — the big house, cars, a boat, success, and fame. I had become a world champion in kart racing and was on track to win at the **NASCAR Cup** level, but I was still empty inside. I lost my wife and child to divorce and began wondering what the real purpose of life was.

God spoke to me and said, *The answer is in the Bible. Read it!*

Through the Bible, I learned that true success is having a personal relationship with the one and only true God. I have found real peace in following him, and he put my life back together. The life I have today is full and complete with family, friends, and a great church. But most importantly, I look forward to spending eternity in heaven with my Lord.

Lake Speed

World Karting Champion and Former NASCAR Driver

The unfolding of your words gives light;
it gives understanding to the simple.

Psalm 119:130

Everything that was written in the past was written to teach us,
so that through endurance and the encouragement of the
Scriptures we might have hope.

Romans 15:4

We have the word of the prophets made more certain, and you will
do well to pay attention to it, as to a light shining in a dark place,
until the day dawns and the morning star rises in your hearts.

2 Peter 1:19

The man who looks intently into the perfect law that gives
freedom, and continues to do this, not forgetting what he has
heard,
but doing it — he will be blessed in what he does.

James 1:25

The racing career of this former **NASCAR** driver began at the age of thirteen, when **Lake Speed** began racing karts. Eventually becoming a six-time United States Karting Champion, he went on to become the World Karting Champion in 1978. Lake then chose to tackle **NASCAR** racing, saying, "It was the highest mountain to climb." Racing in a total of 402 races over nineteen years, he was a top-ten finisher seventy-five times, winning the TranSouth 500 race in 1988.

Today Lake is the vice chairman of **NASCAR** Motor Racing Outreach, whose mission is to introduce the racing community to personal faith in Christ. This ministry is committed to leading others to grow in Christlikeness and stresses involvement in the church to develop meaningful, supportive relationships. It also emphasizes the importance of the believer growing in the knowledge of God's Word, and it assists in the development of leadership skills.

The best advice I ever got ...

Don't ever feel that you are better than someone just because that person is poor.

I was born into a very poor family, the middle child among my four siblings. My father was a mechanic, but we didn't own a car until I was almost twelve years old. One day while we were living in the mountains of California, my father came home with the new car. While we were riding along, I noticed a woman with her three children. They looked very poor to me.

I leaned toward the front seat and said, "Look, Daddy. That lady is staring at our new car!"

That is when my dad instructed me that I should never feel that I was better than someone because that person is poor. I was shocked and embarrassed because I didn't feel that way at all. Nevertheless, I will never forget his lesson. It taught me never to be arrogant or flaunt my success. Rather, I have always shared the blessings of my achievements with others. I have also taught this lesson to my children, who have been so very good to pass it along to their children.

Samuel J. Butcher

Artist and Creator of Precious Moments

As for the rich in this world, charge them not to be proud and
arrogant and contemptuous of others, nor to set their hopes
on uncertain riches, but on God, Who richly and ceaselessly
provides us with everything for [our] enjoyment.

1 Timothy 6:17 AMP

You will be made rich in every way so that you
can be generous on every occasion, and through us
your generosity will result in thanksgiving to God.

2 Corinthians 9:11

Do not think of yourself more highly than you ought,
but rather think of yourself with sober judgment,
in accordance with the measure of faith God has given you.

Romans 12:3

Do nothing out of selfish ambition or vain conceit. Rather, in
humility value others above yourselves.

Philippians 2:3 TNIV

At an early age, **Samuel J. Butcher's** artistic talent was apparent. Because his family was poor, however, drawing materials were scarce. Sam often scoured a nearby factory dump for paper for drawing.

During his school years, Sam won awards for his artwork, but it didn't fill the emptiness he felt inside. Then one night Sam heard the Good News of salvation, and he immediately responded. That decision was followed by a commitment to only use his talent for the Lord.

In 1975, Precious Moments was introduced to the public. The success, however, still did not satisfy Sam because he had a desire to honor the Lord by building the Precious Moments Chapel. Since the structure's initial completion in 1989, millions of visitors have traveled to Carthage, Missouri, to admire Sam's work.

"I see the chapel as an avenue through which I can share my faith," he says. "It is my prayer that the Spirit of God will touch the visitors' hearts and bring them to the saving knowledge of Jesus Christ, our Lord."

The best advice I ever got ...

Ask yourself, "What am I doing with what I've got?"

I received this advice while listening to the sermon my pastor, Dr. Donald V. Wideman, preached almost twenty years ago. Little did I realize what a lasting impact it would have on my life and work.

Just when I start thinking, *If I only had... I could...*, I invariably ask myself, *What am I doing with what I've got?* That changes my perspective completely. I begin to focus on what I have rather than what I lack.

As a marriage-and-family-life instructor, this encourages me daily to use the resources at hand to help students *experience* learning, instead of just giving them information. As a wife and mother, it has become my habit to pray, "Lord, show me how to use what I have in a creative way to make the common extraordinary — to show your love, hospitality, peace, and glory. Amen."

Zeta C. Davidson
Marriage and Family Expert

LORD, you have assigned me my
portion and my cup;
you have made my lot secure.
The boundary lines have fallen
for me in pleasant places;
surely I have a delightful inheritance.
Psalm 16:5–6

We have different gifts, according to the grace given to each of us. If your gift is prophesying, then prophesy in accordance with your faith; if it is serving, then serve; if it is teaching, then teach; if it is to encourage, then give encouragement; if it is giving, then give generously; if it is to lead, do it diligently; if it is to show mercy, do it cheerfully.
Romans 12:6–8 TNIV

No matter what you do, work at it with all your might.
Ecclesiastes 9:10 NIrV

Zeta C. Davidson has a vast and practical knowledge of family dynamics. For twenty-five years, she taught classes on marriage and family to eleventh and twelfth graders in the North Kansas City School District, and she is currently serving on the Board of Directors for the Missouri Educators of Family and Consumer Sciences.

Active in her church, Zeta has led or been involved with numerous committees through the years. She has facilitated Bible studies for engaged and newly married couples, conducted marriage and family seminars, and contributed articles to publications such as *Home Life* and *Living with Children*.

The best advice I ever got ...

Learn the truth:
We all live under grace and
do the best we can.

My father, Billy Graham, made this statement to me at a time when my life was in shambles. I had fled my second marriage in fear for my safety and was full of guilt and shame, feeling I had "out-sinned" God's grace.

I had written a letter to my then-husband and wanted to pass it by my parents for their advice. They listened as I read tearfully of my failure. I had let my family down, and the weight of that was bearing down on me.

When I finished, I looked up at Daddy. He was looking at me tenderly but very seriously. He didn't speak right away, but then said, "Don't be so hard on yourself, Ruth. We all live under grace and do the best we can."

He didn't blame me or say, "I told you so." He spoke words of grace and healing and demonstrated that grace to me. He gave me a safe place to pick up the pieces of my life.

My father's simple statement taught me to extend grace to myself and others. It enables me to share my life transparently with others so that they, too, may understand the goodness of God's outrageous grace.

Ruth Graham

Author, Speaker, and Founder of Ruth Graham and Friends

[God] does not treat us as our sins deserve
or repay us according to our iniquities.
For as high as the heavens are above the earth,
so great is his love for those who fear him;
as far as the east is from the west,
so far has he removed our transgressions from us.
Psalm 103:10–12

From his fullness we have all received, and grace upon grace.
John 1:16 NASB

Let us then approach the throne of grace with confidence, so that
we may receive mercy and find grace to help us in our time of need.
Hebrews 4:16

In [Jesus Christ] we have redemption through his blood,
the forgiveness of sins, in accordance with the riches
of God's grace that he lavished on us.
Ephesians 1:7–8

Author of *In Every Pew Sits a Broken Heart*, **Ruth Graham,** the third child of **Ruth** and **Billy Graham,** seeks to minister God's mercy, grace, restoration, and healing to those who are hurting and feel alone. No stranger to pain, she brings a new and biblical perspective to her journey of faith that took her through her husband's infidelity, her depression, divorces, going back to school at the age of forty, and a variety of life-changing events in the lives of her children.

An articulate and candid speaker, Ruth's transparency enables her to connect with her audiences wherever she goes. She believes that God has given her a unique voice to minister to those who feel marginalized.

Ruth worked in the publishing field for thirteen years as an acquisitions editor and has published several books, including *Legacy of Love ... Things I Learned from My Mother, Legacy of Faith ... Things I Learned from My Father*, **and co-authored** *I'm Pregnant ... Now What?* **and** *So You Want to Adopt* **with Dr. Sara Dormon.**

The best advice I ever got ...

1. Go into business for yourself.

2. You can do it.

3. Keep your faith.

These simple statements made by my father have proven to be invaluable to me, and I attribute much of my success to their wisdom.

The only thing that stands between a man and what he wants from life is often merely the will to try it and the faith to believe that it is possible. Unfortunately, the easiest thing to find on God's green earth is someone to tell you all the things you cannot do. But my father instilled a "can do" spirit in me, and I came to believe that I could go into business for myself and be successful. As a result, I founded several companies. The last one, Amway Corporation (now Alticor, Inc.), hit $6.4 billion for the year in 2004. Through it all, God has helped me to keep my faith strong.

Richard DeVos Sr.

Entrepreneur, Author, Speaker, ...

Jesus said, "All things are possible with God."
Mark 10:27

Lead a life worthy of the calling to which you have been called.
Ephesians 4:1 NRSV

You must make every effort to support your faith with goodness,
and goodness with knowledge, and knowledge with self-control,
and self-control with endurance, and endurance with godliness,
and godliness with mutual affection, and mutual affection with
love. For if these things are yours and are increasing among
you, they keep you from being ineffective and unfruitful in the
knowledge of our Lord Jesus Christ.
2 Peter 1:5–7 NRSV

Just as you received Christ Jesus as Lord, continue to live your
lives in him, rooted and built up in him, strengthened in the faith.
Colossians 2:6–7 TNIV

Probably best known as one of the founders of Amway, now Alticor, **Richard DeVos Sr.** is also the owner and chairman of the Orlando Magic basketball team. He ranks in the Forbes 400, is one of the world's most successful entrepreneurs, and has authored three books. He has been the recipient of numerous achievement awards, as well as eleven honorary doctorate degrees.

DeVos is a popular inspirational and motivational speaker; a community and political leader; and — with his wife, Helen — a generous philanthropist. Because of their dedication to supporting those organizations they believe in, DeVos and his wife created the Richard and Helen DeVos Foundation. The DeVoses are dedicated to making a difference in peoples' lives and to helping people help themselves.

The best advice I ever got ...

Go to college!

After returning from the Navy, I went to see an executive in a large company in hope of securing a job there. I knew the man because my grandparents worked on his estate as caretakers.

During my interview, Mr. Elliott said, "You need to go to college." I was surprised because I had graduated valedictorian of my class, and felt I presented myself well. I hadn't considered college because I was the oldest of seven children, first in my family line to graduate from high school, and no one in our family had gone to college. Also, my father was unemployed, and I had been assisting the family financially since age thirteen.

Mr. Elliott remained insistent in his advice, although he did give me a job as a salesman. I quickly observed, however, that college graduates were promoted ahead of me. A decade later — at age thirty-two — I followed Mr. Elliott's advice and enrolled in college. After graduating with honors, I went on to graduate from seminary magna cum laude and served as a minister and denomination executive for many years. I will always be grateful for Mr. Elliott's stern counsel that broadened my vision and opened a whole new world to me.

Donald V. Wideman

Pastor and Denomination Executive

*Apply your heart to instruction
and your ears to words of knowledge.*
Proverbs 23:12

*Listen to advice and accept instruction,
and in the end you will be wise.*
Proverbs 19:20

*My son, do not forget my teaching,
but keep my commands in your heart,
for they will prolong your life many years
and bring you prosperity.*
Proverbs 3:1–2

*The heart of the discerning acquires knowledge;
the ears of the wise seek it out.*
Proverbs 18:15

Donald V. Wideman served as executive director of the Missouri Baptist Convention from 1987 to 1997. As executive director, Wideman was responsible for the programs that supported the work of more than 600,000 members in 1,900 Southern Baptist churches in Missouri. From 1997–2003, he served as executive director of the Partee Center for Baptist Historical Studies.

In the course of his career, Wideman was the pastor of several churches in Missouri and active at all levels of denominational life in the Southern Baptist Convention, including serving as president. He has been a trustee of Baptist Memorial Hospital, Kansas City, Missouri; William Jewell College, Liberty, Missouri; and Southwestern Baptist Theological Seminary, Fort Worth, Texas.

The best advice I ever got ...

Just be honest and be humble.

This advice was given to me by my dear friend J. B. Fuqua, one of America's most famous entrepreneurs and wisest businessmen. As a member of my board of directors, J. B. was a person I trusted and relied on when I needed wise counsel.

J. B.'s words of wisdom came at a time when I was faced with a confusing and complex crisis, and I have lived by them ever since.

Every successful person reaches a point when he or she is tempted to do or say something they know is wrong in order to get ahead — but it's never worth it in the end. Dishonesty will eat at you and eventually destroy the joy your success should bring. The same is true of pride. It can nullify your success and leave you with nothing. Honesty and humility will never fail you. They will help you reach your goals with dignity, integrity, and the respect of others.

Robert H. Schuller

Pastor, Author, and Motivational Speaker

We . . . aim to be honest and absolutely above suspicion, not only in the sight of the Lord but also in the sight of men.

2 Corinthians 8:21 AMP

The Most High God is like a shield that keeps me safe.
He saves those whose hearts are honest.

Psalm 7:10 NIrV

Jesus said, "Those who exalt themselves will be humbled, and those who humble themselves will be exalted."

Matthew 23:12 TNIV

[God] leads the humble in what is right, and the humble He teaches His way.

Psalm 25:9 AMP

Schuller knew all his life that he wanted to be a minister, and he fulfilled that dream in 1950 when he was ordained by the Reformed Church in America. In 1955, Reverend and Mrs. Robert H. Schuller arrived in Southern California with nothing but a dream in their hearts and five hundred dollars in their pocket. Their dream: "To build a great church for God, a church that would change and save lives, a church dedicated to the creed, 'Find a need and fill it, find a hurt and heal it.'"

Today that church is known as the Crystal Cathedral of Garden Grove, California.

Schuller's positive message of "possibility thinking" has inspired many through his nationally televised weekly program, *The Hour of Power*, and more than thirty books, including five that have appeared on the *New York Times* bestseller list.

The best advice I ever got ...

Only worry about the things that you can control and leave everything else to the Lord.

Back in my college days, I wanted desperately to become the starting quarterback at the University of Miami. When it didn't happen, I struggled with disappointment. I couldn't seem to let it go until the Lord showed me that pining over what I could not change would leave me bitter and jeopardize my future. I needed to trust that his plan was best for me. He urged me to work hard, control my attitude, and trust in him. This enabled me to regain my focus and receive his peace.

So many things happen in life over which we have no control, and it is pointless to waste time and energy worrying about them. As I am faithful to do my part — by being diligent and keeping a positive attitude — and I trust God to take care of the rest, I find that I am free to live life to the fullest.

Mark Richt

Two-Time College Football Coach of the Year

*Trust in the L*ORD *with all your heart*
and lean not on your own understanding;
in all your ways acknowledge him,
and he will make your paths straight.
Proverbs 3:5–6

Do not be anxious about anything, but in everything, by prayer and petition, with thanksgiving, present your requests to God. And the peace of God, which transcends all understanding, will guard your hearts and your minds in Christ Jesus.
Philippians 4:6–7

*I trust in you, O L*ORD;
I say, "You are my God."
My times are in your hands.
Psalm 31:14–15

After five years heading up the Georgia Bulldog program, **Mark Richt** has made it clear that winning with consistency will be a standard for years to come. In five seasons, his Georgia teams have won three SEC Eastern Division titles, two SEC championships, and his 52–13 record is sixth best in the country since 2001. He was named SEC Coach of the Year in 2002 and 2005.

Not only does Richt coach his players on the field, he also strives to teach them godly principles so that they can become better men. His own life serves as a shining example and inspiration. Richt and his wife, Katharyn, have four children, two of whom they adopted from a Ukrainian orphanage, a desire born as a result of a Sunday school lesson on caring for those in need.

Both on the field as a football coach and off the field as a husband and father, Mark Richt's desire is to serve God by serving the people instead of himself.

The best advice I ever got ...

Humility is
the mark of a true winner.

I received this advice in high school from Coach Siesky, one of the winningest coaches in the history of Indiana track and field. It was the first meet of my sophomore year. I had done well the previous season, but I knew I could accomplish more and trained rigorously to do so.

When I finished in first place, I pumped my fist in the air and raised my finger to signal my first victory. I was shocked, however, to see a picture of this in the local paper the next morning. Even though it hadn't been my intention, it looked as if I was signaling that *I* was number one.

That day is when Coach Siesky offered his words of wisdom. He taught me that humility is the mark of a true winner. That season I went on to win all but four meets; I set and broke the city record twice and was named to the all-state team. My picture appeared in the paper five more times, but never again with my finger raised.

Jason Cullum

Minister and Author

Better to be lowly in spirit and among the oppressed
than to share plunder with the proud.
Proverbs 16:19

Pride goes before destruction,
a haughty spirit before a fall.
Proverbs 16:18

Humility and the fear of the LORD
bring wealth and honor and life.
Proverbs 22:4

A man's pride brings him low,
but a man of lowly spirit gains honor.
Proverbs 29:23

Jason Cullum is the executive minister at Christ's Church in Jacksonville, Florida, a multi-campus ministry. He spent the first seven years of his ministry working with children and teens and has an intense passion for developing creative environments for their church experience. He has written articles on family and children's ministry as well as on leadership and technology for several Christian and ministry-related periodicals. He is also in the process of completing his first book, *The Foot Philosophy*, a fable that demonstrates the importance of servant leadership in the marketplace, home, and church. His consulting website is located at www.TheFissionGroup.com.

Growing up in Evansville, Indiana, Jason draws many life lessons from his adolescent adventures along the banks of the Ohio River. Upon receiving a track scholarship, he attended Indiana University. After completing his freshman year, however, his fire for ministry was ignited, and he quickly transferred to Kentucky Christian University where he studied ministry and biblical studies.

The best advice I ever got . . .

When possible, don't be the bearer of bad news.

My friend and mentor Florence Littauer gave me this wise counsel when I related a story to her that began sixteen years before. I had delivered bad news to a person who upon receiving it detested me for it. When she asked me specifically if I knew certain things, I told her the truth, thinking it would help clear up an unsettling situation. I thought I was being a friend. However, the woman was not prepared to hear the truth. All these years later, she still sees me through the lens of that hurtful information.

I am very careful to remember that my calling is to share the Good News, not the current affairs of others. Also I've learned that I can't trust my feelings to determine my actions; I must instead rely on God's leading.

I lost a friend, which is a dear price to pay to learn an important lesson, but I have never forgotten it. I hope it will serve as a "head's up" to others and prevent them from making the same mistake.

Patsy Clairmont

Author and Women of Faith Speaker

Heaviness in the heart of man maketh it stoop:
but a good word maketh it glad.
Proverbs 12:25 KJV

Let your conversation be always full of grace, seasoned with salt.
Colossians 4:6

The mouth of the righteous is a fountain of life.
Proverbs 10:11

Let no unwholesome word proceed from your mouth, but only
such a word as is good for edification according to the need of the
moment, so that it will give grace to those who hear.
Ephesians 4:29 NASB

Petite, profound, and playful. These words help to describe **Patsy Clairmont's** size, message, and humor. This light touch combined with scriptural knowledge makes Patsy an unusual package. Through her message, you find yourself laughing God's truths right into your heart.

Patsy comes from an uncommon background. Her years of suffering as a prisoner in her own home, a victim of agoraphobia, have given her a deep appreciation for God's healing power. God has pulled together the emotionally fragmented pieces of her life and has combined her humor and knowledge of his Word to remind people that imperfect, "cracked" Christians are God's specialty. Whether she is speaking at a Women of Faith conference or writing one of her many bestselling books, Patsy has a way of teaching truth through rib-tickling stories that encourage and heal.

The best advice I ever got ...

Resolve creative differences with inspiration rather than criticism and complaint.

It was Senior Story Artist Joe Ranft who taught me this "no complaint" approach to guiding a creative collaboration: Rather than complaining about ungodly or poorly written and poorly conceived material, redirect the concept to a more acceptable level by enthusiastically inspiring collaborators to achieve the highest standards of excellence.

As I worked alongside Joe—my mentor and friend—I noticed how he inspired and motivated me to present strong, creative ideas and work toward concepts with value and character. He served as an example of genius in the story process.

God has given each of us specific gifts and talents, and we can use them to create concepts that outshine and rise above the rude and crude—without complaining.

Matthew Luhn

Pixar Story Artist

Do everything without complaining or arguing, so that you may become blameless and pure, children of God without fault in a crooked and depraved generation, in which you shine like stars in the universe.

Philippians 2:14–15

Jesus said, "You are the light of the world. A city on a hill cannot be hidden. Neither do people light a lamp and put it under a bowl. Instead they put it on its stand, and it gives light to everyone in the house. In the same way, let your light shine before men, that they may see your good deeds and praise your Father in heaven."

Matthew 5:14–16

Remember the Barbie tour guide in *Toy Story 2* or the scene where the toys cross the street hiding under traffic cones? Just thinking about them probably brings a smile to your face. Who is responsible for such laughter-inspiring genius? Meet **Matthew Luhn**, Pixar story artist.

As a nineteen-year-old animator attracting the attention of Disney, Spielberg, and George Lucas, Luhn began questioning the meaning of life. Then his girlfriend became more serious about her Christian faith, which put a strain on their relationship since Luhn was Jewish. Eventually the girl's pastor met with him. "He showed me all the Old Testament prophecies of who the Messiah would be and lined them up next to the New Testament fulfillments." After taking a year to read the Bible and research Judaism, Christianity, and other faiths, Luhn came to the conclusion that Jesus was indeed the Messiah and he received Christ.

Today, Matthew Luhn helps to craft stories that harmonize with his convictions as a believer—shining a light in a world that can be very dark.

The best advice I ever got ...

Live a legacy.
Have a five-hundred-year
plan for your life.

This statement was made by the speaker of a conference I attended in 1990. From what I could tell, this gentleman was not a Christian, and yet I saw in him the ability to dream bigger than I had ever dared. I sensed the Holy Spirit rise up in me with a holy boldness. If an unbeliever could dream that big, why couldn't I! After all, I'm a servant of God Almighty! It caused me to enlarge my vision and my faith.

Thinking of Isaiah 54:2–3, I began asking God to stretch the boundaries of my tent and to help me see with eternal vision. Shortly after that, I began speaking internationally and have now spoken before government officials, kings, and judges in North America, Central America, Asia, Europe, and Africa. I began "legacy living," working toward a dream that is bigger than one lifetime or even five lifetimes. I no longer settle for mere temporal triumphs. None of us should — our God is an awesome, eternal God.

David Dyson

Educator and Administrator

Enlarge the place of your tent,
*   stretch your tent curtains wide,*
do not hold back;
*   lengthen your cords,*
*   strengthen your stakes.*
For you will spread out to the right and to the left;
*   your descendants will dispossess nations*
*   and settle in their desolate cities.*
Isaiah 54:2–3

This is what the LORD says, he who made the earth, the LORD
who formed it and established it—the LORD is his name:
"Call to me and I will answer you and tell you great and
unsearchable things you do not know."
Jeremiah 33:2–3

I pray also that the eyes of your heart may be enlightened in order
that you may know the hope to which he has called you, the riches
of his glorious inheritance in the saints, and his incomparably
great power for us who believe.
Ephesians 1:18–19

David Dyson has served on the administrative staff of **Oral Roberts University** in **Tulsa, Oklahoma,** for twenty-six years, nine of those as the dean of the **School of Business.** His honors include being named to *Who's Who Among America's Teachers*, *Who's Who in Finance and Industry*, **and** *Who's Who in American Education.*

Dyson earned his doctorate at the **University of Arkansas, Fayetteville,** in **Strategic Human Resource Management. Graduating with honors, he earned an MBA at Oral Roberts University. Dyson is a member of the Academy of Management and has written and developed more than twenty scholarly articles and presentations. In addition, he has made professional presentations in several African nations, Albania, Canada, India, and Mexico.**

The best advice I ever got ...

Don't stop dancing with the one who brought you to the prom.

This advice was given to me by my husband, Randy. He used the phrase to encourage me to maintain the foundation and fundamentals that helped to create my success.

I am often reminded of this wisdom when multiple options have been presented during seasons of accelerated growth, achievement, and success.

This wise counsel has kept me grounded and helped me to stay true to my core values. When it comes to making decisions, I keep these things in mind, and it makes it much easier to eliminate the options that don't fit.

Paula White

Pastor, Motivational Speaker, and Author

It is required that those who have been
given a trust must prove faithful.
1 Corinthians 4:2

Jesus said, "I will show you what he is like who comes to
me and hears my words and puts them into practice. He is
like a man building a house, who dug down deep and laid the
foundation on rock. When a flood came, the torrent struck that
house but could not shake it, because it was well built."
Luke 6:47–48

Who then is the faithful and wise servant, whom the master has
put in charge of the servants in his household to give them their
food at the proper time? It will be good for that servant whose
master finds him doing so when he returns. I tell you the truth,
he will put him in charge of all his possessions.
Matthew 24:45–47

Until the age of five, **Paula White** had a typical childhood, including a loving family and stable home life. Then tragedy struck: her father committed suicide. The unthinkable became worse when Paula's cries for love were muffled by years of sexual and physical abuse from the ages of six to thirteen.

At the age of eighteen, Paula was introduced to Jesus Christ. Who would have ever dreamed that in time she would grace the covers of major magazines, be featured by international media, and dialogue with leaders like Colin Powell, Margaret Thatcher, Benjamin Netanyahu, and Presidents George H. W. and George W. Bush?

Today, Paula White is an inspiration to millions around the world who seek God's love. She co-pastors the 22,000-member Without Walls International Church in Tampa with her husband, Randy, hosts an international television program, spearheads humanitarian efforts worldwide, and all while traveling the world fulfilling her mission and call to "transform lives, heal hearts, and win souls."

The best advice I ever got ...

Only those who try succeed.

It's true — every single person who has ever succeeded started out by trying. And it is a guarantee that if you don't try, you won't succeed.

My mother often told my siblings and me this as we were growing up. She encouraged us to use our gifts and "go for it," even when conventional wisdom said that it was crazy. For that reason, my creative brother is a successful, working actor; my math-minded sister is a successful actuary with her own business; and I am a successful writer with more than sixty books published.

Growing up, I never thought twice about trying something that was hard. When I first told people I wanted to be a writer, some laughed and rolled their eyes. They didn't know anyone who'd ever done that, so they assumed that it was just a pipe dream. But I decided to try anyway.

Over the years I've talked to many people who have expressed the desire to be a writer but never got past the wishing stage and actually tried. Needless to say, those people didn't succeed. Trying doesn't always guarantee success, but the odds are a lot better for those who do!

Terri Blackstock

Bestselling Author of Christian Novels

The Lord says,
"Do not be afraid—I am with you!
I am your God—let nothing terrify you!
I will make you strong and help you."
Isaiah 41:10 GNT

The plans of people who work hard succeed.
Proverbs 21:5 NIrV

May the favor of the Lord our God rest upon us;
establish the work of our hands for us—
yes, establish the work of our hands.
Psalm 90:17

Commit to the LORD everything you do.
Then your plans will succeed.
Proverbs 16:3 NIrV

Just ten years ago, **Terri Blackstock** was an award-winning secular novelist writing for publishers such as HarperCollins, Harlequin, and Silhouette. With thirty-two titles published and 3.5 million books in print, she found that the compromises she had made in her career had taken their toll on her spiritual life, and she yearned to get back into a right relationship with Christ. After much soul-searching, she decided that she would never write another thing that didn't glorify God.

Since then, Terri has published more than twenty-five novels, many of which have been bestsellers. She writes about flawed Christians in crisis and about God's provision for their mistakes and wrong choices. While most of her novels are in the mystery/suspense genre, she has also rewritten four of her earlier books as Christian romances. In addition, she is co-author of a series of family values novels with Beverly LaHaye. Three of her latest works have held number-one spots on the bestseller lists.

The best advice I ever got ...

Go where God calls you. He wants you more than your money.

I had just finished directing the turnaround of a major division of the multibillion-dollar company I was working for, and the **CEO** asked me to take on another similar assignment. At the same time, I was invited to leave that company and lead a ministry-related for-profit company. Although the new opportunity was smaller than my prior assignments and the pay was substantially less, I sensed an urging from God to consider it.

As I prayed, I also consulted two trusted friends — my former minister (and good friend) and a vice president of a major automotive company who was also a good friend. I told them of the opportunity and that it would mean much lower compensation and significantly reduce my ability to give to God's work. These Christian men both had the same advice: "Go where God calls you. He wants you more than your money."

By accepting God's call, I was instrumental in another "turnaround." The effort was not without challenge, but a valuable company was able to have a positive impact on the culture of the world.

James Buick

Business Executive

To obey is better than sacrifice.
1 Samuel 15:22

Teach me to do your will,
for you are my God.
Let your good spirit lead me
on a level path.
Psalm 143:10 NRSV

It is God who is at work in you, enabling you both
to will and to work for his good pleasure.
Philippians 2:13 NRSV

The world and its desires pass away,
but the man who does the will of God lives forever.
1 John 2:17

Jim Buick worked with Dearborn Machinery Movers, Clark Equipment Company, Brunswick Corporation, and Ford Motor Company before taking the helm at Zondervan in 1984. A savvy financial mind, he helped the publishing company rise from disarray and engineered its purchase by HarperCollins in 1988.

Now retired, he serves on the Board of Directors for four companies and consults for two-dozen more — that's when he isn't writing and speaking on business issues and life planning.

Another activity close to his heart stems from his own experience with a personal life planner. After taking extensive training, Jim now meets with men in transition one-on-one and helps them develop personal Life Plans.

The best advice I ever got ...

If you're going to do it, do it right.

I heard these words many times as I worked with my dad in his home redecorating business. I loved working with him because even before I became a teenager, he would let me do things generally done by adults. The only catch was, if I was going to do a man's work, I had to work like a man. That meant that many times my perfectionist dad insisted that I redo projects until I got them right. To this day, I can still hear his advice ringing in my ears.

I saw this attitude of excellence personified in the late Dale Earnhardt when I worked for his organization. One day a female employee was having trouble with her car and "Big E" happened to pass by. Rather than call one of his mechanics, he crawled into the car himself and stayed on task until he determined the problem and fixed it. His attitude was, if you want something done right, you throw yourself completely into the situation and stay after it until you are satisfied that the undertaking has been accomplished successfully.

In my own life — whether at home, in my marriage, raising my children, at work, or in my ministry — I am responsible to put forth my best effort.

Jim Coté

Author, Speaker, and Corporate Chaplain

Whatever your hand finds to do, do it with all your might.
Ecclesiastes 9:10

Whatever you do, work at it with all your heart,
as working for the Lord, not for men, since you know
that you will receive an inheritance from the Lord as a reward.
It is the Lord Christ you are serving.
Colossians 3:23–24

Do your best to present yourself to God as one approved,
a workman who does not need to be ashamed.
2 Timothy 2:15

Jim Coté is the founder and president of The Master's Men Ministry, whose mission is to help "build noble men" by providing a place for men to discuss men's issues and discover biblical solutions for the challenges they face. The ministry uses athletic outreach events to both entertain and introduce men to one another in the ministry. Also, men are invited to attend one of the Master's Men groups in their area, where discussion, prayer, and biblical principles are sought for individual encouragement and guidance.

Ordained in 1989, Jim served as the corporate chaplain for Interstate Battery Systems of America for ten years. He then went on to direct the chaplains of Motor Racing Outreach — a ministry to motor sport professionals — where he served until 2000. The author of two books, Jim has ministered to men for more than twenty years, while providing spiritual leadership to athletic professionals in a variety of sports.

The best advice I ever got ...

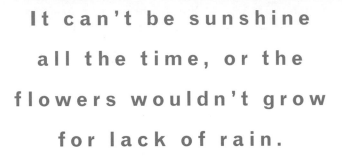

It can't be sunshine all the time, or the flowers wouldn't grow for lack of rain.

My mother wrote these words of wisdom to me in a letter during my college years when I was struggling. I was working part time and having difficulty completing my courses, and her timely encouragement gave me the fresh perspective and boost I needed.

I've never forgotten those important words. They have carried me through many trials over the years. What I have learned is that there is no achievement without struggle. The Lord uses trials and trouble to draw us to him and to teach us to rely on his strength rather than our own. He develops our character and faith through all the difficulties of life on this earth.

Francine Rivers

Author

All things work together and are [fitting into a plan]
for good to and for those who love God and are called
according to [His] design and purpose.
Romans 8:28 AMP

You will face all kinds of trouble. When you do, think of it as
pure joy. Your faith will be put to the test. You know that when
that happens it will produce in you the strength to continue. The
strength to keep going must be allowed to finish its work. Then you
will be all you should be. You will have everything you need.
James 1:2–4 NIrV

The Lord said to me, "My grace is sufficient for you, for my power
is made perfect in weakness." . . . That is why, for Christ's sake, I
delight in weaknesses, in insults, in hardships, in persecutions, in
difficulties. For when I am weak, then I am strong.
2 Corinthians 12:9–10

Francine Rivers has been writing for more than twenty years. From 1976 to 1985, she had a successful writing career in the general market and won numerous awards. After becoming a Christian in 1986, Francine wrote *Redeeming Love* as her statement of faith.

Since then, Francine has published numerous books and has continued to win both industry acclaim and reader loyalty. Her novel *The Last Sin Eater* won the ECPA Gold Medallion, and three of her books have won the prestigious Romance Writers of America Rita Award.

Francine uses her writing to draw closer to the Lord, that through her work she might worship and praise Jesus for all he has done and is doing in her life.

The best advice I ever got . . .

If every day was a good day, there would be no good days.

Believe it or not, these life-changing words came to me on the bottle cap of the Nantucket Nectar I was drinking. Ever since, this saying has become my personal mantra. Not bad for a bottle cap!

All of us want every day to be a good day, but it's the bad days that help us appreciate the good days! Sickness helps us appreciate health. Failure helps us appreciate success. Debt helps us appreciate wealth. And the tough times help us appreciate the good times.

July 23, 2000, was the worst day of my life. My intestines ruptured, and I should have died. I lost twenty-five pounds in one week, spent two days on a respirator, and now have an eighteen-inch scar on my abdomen.

It was the worst day of my life, but I can honestly say that it was the best day of my life as well. I wouldn't trade the lessons I've learned from that experience for anything in the world. I have an intense appreciation for life that few people can comprehend.

So whether we are having a good day or a bad day, we can remind ourselves that God is God and God is good.

Mark Batterson

Pastor and Author

This is the day the LORD has made;
Let us rejoice and be glad in it.
Psalm 118:24

Everything created by God is good, and nothing is to be rejected,
provided it is received with thanksgiving; for it is sanctified by
God's word and by prayer.
1 Timothy 4:4–5 NRSV

Praise be to the God ... of all comfort, who comforts us in all our
troubles, so that we can comfort those in any trouble with the
comfort we ourselves have received from God.
2 Corinthians 1:3–4

A righteous man may have many troubles,
but the LORD delivers him from them all.
Psalm 34:19

Mark Batterson serves as lead pastor of National Community Church (www.theaterchurch.com) in Washington, **DC**. Targeting emerging generations, 73 percent of **NCC**ers are single twentysomethings that live or work on Capitol Hill.

Starting with a core group of nineteen people, **NCC** has morphed into one church with five services in three locations. In addition, their theaterchurch.com podcast is one of the fastest growing church podcasts in America. The vision of **NCC** is to meet in movie theaters at metro stops throughout the Washington, **DC** area. Currently they are meeting at three such locations, one of which is Union Station.

Mark is the author of *ID: The True You* as well as *In a Pit with a Lion on a Snowy Day.* He is also a daily blogger at www.markbatterson.com.

The best advice I ever got ...

Don't waste your suffering.

I began my career in 1962, and for the first ten years, I could do no wrong. I had a meteoric rise. But when I signed with the Chicago Bulls, things began to change — and not for the better. I was a new Christian at the time, struggling to understand why things were worse instead of better now that I was God's man.

That is when I called Warren Wiersbe, former pastor of Moody Church in Chicago, and asked if we could have lunch. I filled him in. I told him how surprised I was when things started to go wrong, how I had prayed, "Lord, do you remember me? I'm serving you!" Warren answered, "Pat, don't waste your sufferings." I was baffled at his response.

Thirty-four years later, I can appreciate what he said to me. Being a Christian does not mean that we will never have a problem or disappointment. Life — even the life of a Christian — is tough. God expects us to embrace our suffering, learn from it, and let it help us grow. When we do, we become wiser, sharper, and more effective in what God has called us to do. That's the key to the triumphant life.

Pat Williams

Senior Vice President of the NBA's Orlando Magic

The God of all grace, who called
you to his eternal glory in Christ,
after you have suffered a little
while, will himself restore you
and make you strong, firm and
steadfast.

1 Peter 5:10

He helps us in all our troubles,
so that we are able to help others who have
all kinds of troubles, using the same help that
we ourselves have received from God.

2 Corinthians 1:4 GNT

Although [Jesus] was a son, he learned obedience from what he
suffered and, once made perfect, he became the source of eternal
salvation for all who obey him.

Hebrews 5:8–9

We know that in all things God works
for the good of those who love him.

Romans 8:28 NIrV

Pat Williams is the senior vice president of the **NBA's Orlando Magic** and the author of more than forty books. One of America's top motivational, inspirational, and humorous speakers, he has addressed employees from many Fortune 500 companies, the Million Dollar Round Table, two Billy Graham Crusades, two Peter Lowe Success Seminars, and groups on many university campuses.

Since 1968, he has been affiliated with National Basketball Association teams in Chicago, Atlanta, and Philadelphia, including the 1983 World Champion 76ers, and now the Orlando Magic, which he co-founded in 1987 and helped lead to the **NBA** finals in 1995. Twenty-three of his teams have gone to the **NBA** play-offs and five of them have made the **NBA** finals. In 1996, Pat was named as one of the fifty most influential people in **NBA** history by a national publication.

Pat and his wife, Ruth, are the parents of nineteen children, including fourteen adopted from four nations, ranging in age from twenty to thirty-four, and have been featured in many major periodicals and major television networks.

The best advice I ever got ...

Never give in — never, never, never, never, in nothing great or small, large or petty, never give in except to convictions of honor and good sense.

These words were spoken by Winston Churchill in 1941 when he addressed the boys at his alma mater, Harrow School, in England. Although myth has it that these words were the full text of his remarks, they were part of a much longer speech in which he exhorted the students at the height of World War II.

Like many people, I have taken these famous words to be a valuable and important exhortation. With God's help, I have followed them and attribute much of my success to their wisdom.

Jan Karon

Author of the Bestselling Mitford Series

Consider it pure joy, my brothers and sisters, whenever you face trials of many kinds, because you know that the testing of your faith produces perseverance. Let perseverance finish its work so that you may be mature and complete, not lacking anything.

James 1:2–4 TNIV

Let us not lose heart and grow weary and faint in acting nobly and doing right, for in due time and at the appointed season we shall reap, if we do not loosen and relax our courage and faint.

Galatians 6:9 AMP

Blessed are those who persevere under trial, because when they have stood the test, they will receive the crown of life that God has promised to those who love him.

James 1:12 TNIV

We consider blessed those who have persevered. You have heard of Job's perseverance and have seen what the Lord finally brought about. The Lord is full of compassion and mercy.

James 5:11

Jan Karon wrote her first novel at the age of ten. "The manuscript was written on Blue Horse notebook paper, and was, for good reason, kept hidden from my sister. When she found it, she discovered the one curse word I had included. After my grandmother's exceedingly focused reproof, I've written books without cussin' ever since."

Several years ago, Karon left a successful career in advertising to write books. "I stepped out on faith to follow my lifelong dream of being an author," she says. "I made real sacrifices and took big risks. But living, it seems to me, is largely about risk."

Enthusiastic booksellers across the country have introduced readers of all ages to Karon's heartwarming books. *At Home in Mitford*, Karon's first book in the *Mitford* series, was nominated for an ABBY by the American Booksellers Association in 1996, 1997, and 1998.

The best advice I ever got ...

Seek first his kingdom and ... all these things will be given to you.

After earning a master's in business administration and reaching the top of my career within a few short years, I enjoyed professional recognition and many other good "things." Then, in 1974, I had an encounter with the Lord that dramatically changed my life and priorities.

The Lord called me to leave my successful career and all of its security to live a life of faith, totally trusting him to meet our needs. It was during the times of uncertainty that the Lord impressed these words of Jesus from Matthew 6:33 on my heart. That was more than thirty years ago. We have never lacked anything we have needed since that time.

Not only has God given us all we need to fulfill his plan for our lives, but he has also given us more than enough to help many other people along their journeys. He has enabled me to do what he called me to do — which was totally beyond my own ability to accomplish — and has given us many more "things" than we ever thought we would have, certainly more than I was able to provide through my career.

Richard Booker

Minister and Author

Jesus said, "I tell you, do not worry about your life, what you will eat or drink; or about your body, what you will wear. . . . Look at the birds of the air; they do not sow or reap or store away in barns, and yet your heavenly Father feeds them. Are you not much more valuable than they? Who of you by worrying can add a single hour to his life? And why do you worry about clothes? See how the lilies of the field grow. They do not labor or spin. Yet I tell you that not even Solomon in all his splendor was dressed like one of these. If that is how God clothes the grass of the field, which is here today and tomorrow is thrown into the fire, will he not much more clothe you?"

Matthew 6:25–30

My God will meet all your needs according to his glorious riches in Christ Jesus.

Philippians 4:19

The Lord has said,
"If you are willing and obedient,
    you will eat the best from the land."

Isaiah 1:19

Richard Booker, MBA, PhD, is an ordained Christian minister, president of Sounds of the Trumpet, Inc., and the founder/director of the Institute for Hebraic-Christian Studies. He is the author of more than twenty-five books, which have been translated into numerous languages with approximately four hundred thousand copies in print. Richard's seminars and books are unique in that they contain the meat of Scripture in a clear, easy-to-understand language with practical application for everyday Christian living.

Richard and his wife, Peggy, co-founded the Institute for Hebraic-Christian Studies (IHCS) in 1997 as a ministry to educate Christians in the Hebraic culture and background of the Bible, build relationships between Christians and Jews, and give comfort and support to the people of Israel. He has also produced study material on the biblical Hebraic roots of Christianity for homeschoolers.

Richard has a daily television program, which can be seen on the Internet at www.godslearningchannel.com, and he is a spiritual father to many believers around the world.

The best advice I ever got ...

Remember — it's not the college. It's you.

I was making plans to attend a Christian college and was having a difficult time deciding which school would best prepare me for what God wanted me to do in life. My uncle, a missionary in the Yukon, came to say his good-bye before heading back North. Knowing of my struggle, he offered just the words I needed.

It didn't take me long to learn that my uncle's thought applied not only to the college I would choose, but to all of life. As a Christian, there would only be success and peace of heart as I totally relied on God's direction and submitted my life to him. Submission — it sounds so simple, but it is one of the hardest things for us as humans to do. We wish to be in charge of our own decisions and destiny.

Submission doesn't just apply to once-in-a-lifetime things. We need to resubmit our lives with every new situation that we face, saying, "This, too, belongs to you, Lord." It wasn't the college, it isn't my writing, it is only as I submit to God and he is able to direct and use me that any ministry can take place.

Janette Oke

Author

During the days of Jesus' life on earth, he offered
up prayers and petitions with loud cries and tears ...
and he was heard because of his reverent submission.

Hebrews 5:7

Jesus prayed, "Father, ... not my will, but yours be done."

Luke 22:42

God opposes the proud
but shows favor to the humble.

James 4:6 TNIV

He leads the humble in what is right,
and the humble He teaches His way.

Psalm 25:9 AMP

The Lord says, "This is the man to whom I will
look and have regard: he who is humble and ...
who trembles at My word and reveres My commands."

Isaiah 66:2 AMP

Janette Oke (pronounced "oak") pioneered inspirational fiction and is still one of the leading authors in the category today. *Love Comes Softly*, her first novel, has sold more than one million copies. Janette is now the bestselling author of over seventy books, thirty-two of which have been translated into fifteen languages. Her books have sold over thirty million copies.

Janette receives fan mail from all over the world and answers each letter personally. She received the 1992 President's Award from the Evangelical Christian Publishers Association for her significant contribution to Christian fiction, the 1999 CBA Life Impact Award, and has been awarded the Gold Medallion Award and the Christy Award for fiction.

The best advice I ever got . . .

People like people who like what they like.

This wisdom was given to me by the trainer on my first position out of college — sales for a soft drink company. Ron said that if I wanted to be a success, I should concentrate on only one thing: clues. A clue, he said, might be a tie tack, the calendar on the wall, anything that might indicate something the buyer is interested in. "When you talk to someone about something they love, they will include you in their affection. And when people like you, they are much more inclined to help you. After that, sell, advertise, and display. But first look for clues."

It worked. Regardless of the nationality of the customer, their economic status, or the part of town in which they did business, they all responded positively to a kid with little experience who knew how to ask interested questions. A year and a half later, the company promoted me to supervisor.

Many think that they will be well received if they do the talking and are bright and informed on their subject, but actually the opposite is true. I have found that when I ask others' opinions and show enthusiasm about what they say, truly meaningful relationships have developed and that is my key to success.

John Holland
Speaker, Counselor, and Board Executive

Do nothing out of selfish ambition or vain conceit, but in humility consider others better than yourselves. Each of you should look not only to your own interests, but also to the interests of others.

Philippians 2:3–4

Jesus said, "Do to others as you would have them do to you."

Luke 6:31

How good and pleasant it is
when brothers live together in unity!
It is like precious oil poured on the head,
running down on the beard,
running down on Aaron's beard,
down upon the collar of his robes.
It is as if the dew of Hermon
were falling on Mount Zion.
For there the LORD bestows his blessing,
even life forevermore.

Psalm 133

John Holland is a storyteller with a passion for people. In addition to ministering in conferences and seminars across the United States, he and his wife, Doris, counsel pastors, leaders, and couples on marriage.

He holds a Doctor of Divinity from the International Church of the Foursquare Gospel and a Doctor of Letters from Oral Roberts University.

John served as president of the International Church of the Foursquare Gospel and pastor of the headquarters' church, Angelus Temple. In addition, he has served on the executive committee of the Pentecostal Fellowship of North America as well as on the boards of L.I.F.E. Bible College, the American Bible Society, the Pentecostal/Charismatic Churches of North America, and Mission America. He is also listed in *Who's Who in Religion in America*.

The best advice I ever got . . .

1. Trust in the Lord with all your heart.

2. Imitate the Lord in everything you say and do.

3. Keep going, no matter what.

These three instructions have guided me while serving God at home and on foreign soil for three decades.

The first came straight from the most reliable source of advice ever known — the Bible. "Trust in the LORD with all your heart and lean not on your own understanding; in all your ways acknowledge him, and he will make your paths straight" (Proverbs 3:5–6).

The second was given to me by Reverend Bonnie J. Hall, while I was serving under her ministry and pioneering a church. She said, "Imitate the Lord in everything you say, everything you do, and every place you go; and especially keep your eyes on the Master and not pastors. Even well-meaning pastors will at times fail you, but God never will."

The third came from Dr. Pauline Parham, while I was attending Christ for the Nation Institute back in the 1970s. I was to answer God's call to foreign missions. She told us, "When in ministry you will sometimes feel down, deserted, and as though no one cares. Encourage yourself by reaching down, getting hold of your bootstraps, and pulling yourself up. Then keep going, no matter what. If God is for you, who can be against you?"

James Hilton

Minister and Missionary

Jesus said, "I have set you an example
that you should do as I have done for you."
John 13:15

Let us fix our eyes on Jesus, the author
and perfecter of our faith.... Consider him
who endured such opposition from sinful men,
so that you will not grow weary and lose heart.
Hebrews 12:2–3

Why are you downcast, O my soul?
Why so disturbed within me?
Put your hope in God.
Psalm 42:5

God has said,
"I will never leave you.
I will never desert you."
So we can say boldly,
"The Lord helps me. I will not be afraid.
What can a mere man do to me?"
Hebrews 13:5–6 NIrV

James Hilton is founder and president of Message of Faith World Ministries, Inc., a full-gospel interdenominational ministry. He and his wife, Coriene, have ministered in many areas, including pioneering and pastoring churches in the United States and abroad. Along with their evangelistic work, they have written Christian literature, college correspondence courses, children's literature, and the *Mission Manual Instruction Book.*

The Hiltons have extensive experience in establishing, administrating, and directing Bible colleges and have conducted numerous tent evangelism meetings, seminars for pastors, missionary training seminars, and other conventions. In addition, the Hiltons have developed preschools, food and clothing programs, and women's and children's ministries. James has also ministered on radio stations in the United States and in other countries as well as on various television stations, including guest appearances on Celebration Daystar TV.

The best advice I ever got ...

Life is more fulfilling and the heart is freer to be happy when we remain open and aboveboard with Christ.

Those weren't the exact words my mama used, but that was the lesson I learned. When I was about eleven, I went to a friend's house to play one afternoon. The boy said that he wanted to show me a tiny telescope, but when I peered into it, I saw a pornographic picture. Giving in to the pressure of the moment, I laughed, but my conscience was pricked.

The next day, Mama called me into the kitchen. "Jack, I want to ask you a question. But listen carefully because I'm asking you *in front of Jesus*." My heart practically stopped. Instinctively she had known something was wrong when I arrived at home the previous day. With sincere tears, I poured out my heart and asked her to pray with me. Immediately, the sense of uncleanness left, and I was filled with the joyous peace we can all gain *in front of Jesus.* The weight was gone, and I was free.

When my mother said, "in front of Jesus," it was her way of reminding me that life only works right when we shoot straight with God. Through the years, this lesson has enabled me keep "on line" with heaven, so I will be "in line" when my Father God calls me to his forever home. The sum of it all is simple: If I live in front of Jesus here, I will be ready to stand in front of him there. Nothing is more important to me.

Jack W. Hayford
Pastor Emeritus, Church Leader, and Author

If we claim to be without sin, we deceive ourselves and the truth is not in us. If we confess our sins, he is faithful and just and will forgive us our sins and purify us from all unrighteousness.

1 John 1:8–9

I acknowledged my sin to you
and did not cover up my iniquity.
I said, "I will confess
my transgressions to the Lord"—
and you forgave
the guilt of my sin.

Psalm 32:5

He who conceals his sins does not prosper,
but whoever confesses and renounces them finds mercy.

Proverbs 28:13

Jack W. Hayford is president of the International Church of the Foursquare Gospel; founder and chancellor of The King's College and Seminary; and director of The JWH School of Pastoral Nurture. He is most widely known as founding pastor of The Church On The Way, in Van Nuys, California, where he was senior pastor from 1969–1999. Today he still ministers there on occasion as pastor emeritus.

Hayford has authored fifty-two books and written more than four hundred musical works, including the world renowned song "Majesty." He serves on various international/interdenominational committees and councils and is most often referred to as "Pastor Jack" — his preferred title. A nationally and internationally recognized scholar and teacher, Hayford draws on a wealth of experience to mentor other leaders and today is recognized as a "pastor to pastors." His travels and ministry to denominational and interdenominational gatherings have caused Hayford to become an acknowledged bridge-builder — helping to forge healthy bonds among all sectors of the church.

Wait for **God's** best, and seek first the kingdom of **God** and his righteousness.

Years ago, my mother wrote these words to me in a letter, and to this day they guide every decision I make.

Think for a moment and you'll realize that most of the choices that face us are not between "good" and "bad" but between "good" and "best." That's what makes them so difficult. Should I pursue a career in medicine or law? Do I want three children or four? Should I marry this delightful person or that one? Should I attend this great church or the one a mile farther down the road?

God has the answers we seek. He is the one who can help us discern the good path from the best path. Ask him and then listen for his answer. Ask him which would best promote his kingdom.

The decision-making process is tricky. Let God help you see through the fog and choose the most rewarding path on your life's journey.

Angela Thomas

Author and Speaker

Be patient and wait for the Lord to act;
don't be worried about those who prosper
or those who succeed in their evil plans.

Psalm 37:7 GNT

Jesus said, "Put God's kingdom first. Do what he wants you to do. Then all of those things will also be given to you."

Matthew 6:33 NIrV

Do not be conformed to this world (this age), [fashioned after and adapted to its external, superficial customs], but be transformed (changed) by the [entire] renewal of your mind [by its new ideals and its new attitude], so that you may prove [for yourselves] what is the good and acceptable and perfect will of God, even the thing which is good and acceptable and perfect [in His sight for you].

Romans 12:2 AMP

Angela Thomas is both an engaging speaker and a gifted writer. More than anything else, she pours her heart into everything she does. She is the author of more than a dozen books, including: *Tender Mercy for a Mother's Soul*, *An Expectant Mother's Journal*, *Do You Think I'm Beautiful?*, and her newest release, *When Wallflowers Dance*.

Angela is a graduate of Dallas Theological Seminary. Her constant prayer is to live a life in passionate response to God and to help others connect with him, so they can do the same.

The best advice I ever got ...

Always carry yourself with confidence — even when you don't feel confident.

I was just a young teenager when I began to run track internationally and go along on mission trips. My first big trip was to Russia, Poland, and West Germany with the U.S. track team. Before I left, my mother took me aside and said: "Madeline, you must project a level of confidence as you travel. There are unscrupulous people out there who will try to take advantage of you — and they'll succeed if you let them. These people prey on the vulnerable and naive. Even when you don't feel particularly confident, act as if you know exactly what you are doing, and they'll keep their distance."

This advice has helped me greatly in my public life as well as in my travels. I quickly saw that there are people who will try to talk to you, usher you into the wrong car, even push their way into your room. These people are not interested in your message. They just want to take advantage of you in any way they can. I believe that my mother's advice helped keep me safe as I visited many distant places with unfamiliar cultures. I pass this advice on to my students as I serve in my role as high school teacher and coach.

Madeline Manning Mims

Athlete, Minister, and Teacher

You have been my hope, O Sovereign LORD,
my confidence since my youth.

Psalm 71:5

The LORD will be your confidence
and will keep your foot from being snared.

Proverbs 3:26

The fruit of righteousness will be peace;
the effect of righteousness will be quietness and
confidence forever.

Isaiah 32:17

We say with confidence,
"The Lord is my helper; I will not be afraid.
What can man do to me?"

Hebrews 13:6

Named one of America's Outstanding Young Women, **Madeline** is a gold and silver Olympic medalist in track.

She pioneered the 800-meter run for the United States by being the first (and at present) the only American woman to take home the gold in this event. In addition, she holds the American Record, Olympic Record, and World Record in the 800-meter. She has been a member of four U.S. Olympic teams, spanning a sixteen-year international career. Madeline has shared her personal testimony at the White House and on the steps of the Capitol in response to the presidential address to the Olympians and American people. She has been inducted into the National and Olympic Halls of Fame and was honored at the 2000 Sydney Olympic Games as a "legend in the stadium."

Madeline currently teaches Bible and coaches high school track in Tulsa, Oklahoma.

The best advice I ever got ...

He is no fool who gives what he cannot keep to gain what he cannot lose.

Missionary Jim Elliot spoke these words; he lived them. Shortly after answering God's call to carry the gospel to the Huaorani Indians in Ecuador, he and his fellow missionaries were martyred. He did not hesitate to give his life, knowing that he would gain an eternal reward that could not be taken from him.

People often miss the fact that we can't hold on to earthly treasures, whether money, possessions, or time. But if we give them away, investing them in God's kingdom, we'll have the pleasure of helping the needy and reaching the lost, *and* we'll enjoy eternal treasures forever on the New Earth. That's a win/win situation.

We all want gain, but Jim Elliot sought gain that would last forever. That's what I want too. Jesus put it this way, "Store up for yourselves treasures in heaven."

Randy Alcorn
Author and Speaker

Jesus said, "Whoever finds his life will lose it,
and whoever loses his life for my sake will find it."
Matthew 10:39

Jesus said, "Everyone who has left houses or brothers or sisters
or father or mother or children or fields for my sake will receive a
hundred times as much and will inherit eternal life."
Matthew 19:29

Jesus said, "Sell your possessions and give to the poor. Provide
purses for yourselves that will not wear out, a treasure in heaven
that will not be exhausted, where no thief comes near and no moth
destroys. For where your treasure is, there your heart will be also."
Luke 12:33–34

Randy Alcorn is the founder and director of Eternal Perspective Ministries, a nonprofit organization dedicated to teaching biblical truth and drawing attention to and meeting the needs of the unreached, unfed, unborn, uneducated, unreconciled, and unsupported people around the world.

"My focus is communicating the strategic use of our time, money, possessions, and opportunities to invest in need-meeting ministries that count for eternity," Alcorn says.

Before starting **EPM** in 1990, Alcorn co-pastored for thirteen years and ministered in many countries. A popular teacher and conference speaker, he has taught part time at **Western Seminary and Multnomah Bible College.**

Alcorn is the author of twenty books and numerous articles for Christian magazines. In addition, he has been a guest on more than five hundred radio and television programs including *Focus on the Family*.

Once you set your course, keep your eye on the goal and don't let anything distract you. If you get it right the first time, things will line up from there.

My father gave me this advice when I was nine. Sand storms had obliterated our early crops, and my father was forced to take a job in town. Amazingly, I was given the responsibility of plowing the rows and planting the fall crops — our only hope for a late harvest to cover the note on our farm.

I looked across the fields, left barren by the sand, and remembered the straight rows my father had planted. When I asked how I could possibly do that when there were no old rows to go by, my father answered, "See that post at the far end of the field? Guide the tractor straight for it. If a gnat flies into your ear or a bird flies across your path, don't take your eyes off that post. If you can do that, you will set the first row properly and the others will be easy after that."

Each time I come to a place in life where I don't know how I will properly accomplish what God is asking me to do, I remember my dad's advice. I set a manageable goal and keep my eyes on that goal. No matter what happens, I don't let myself get distracted. After I reach that first goal, things are much easier.

Dwyan Calvert

General Manager and Pastor

I do not consider myself yet to have taken hold of it. But one thing I
do: Forgetting what is behind and straining toward what is ahead, I
press on toward the goal to win the prize for which God has called
me heavenward in Christ Jesus.
Philippians 3:13–14

Be firm (steadfast), immovable,
always abounding in the work of the Lord.
1 Corinthians 15:58 AMP

That enemy of yours, the devil, roams around like a lion roaring
[in fierce hunger], seeking someone to seize upon and devour.
Withstand him; be firm in faith [against his onset — rooted,
established, strong, immovable, and determined].
1 Peter 5:8–9 AMP

Dwyan Calvert is the founder and general manager of **KSWP (90.9)** and **KAVX (91.9)** in Lufkin, Texas. **KSWP** (Christian Music for Your Family) went on the air in 1984. It is now the most listened to Christian radio station in **East Texas**, four times named a finalist for Station of the Year (Small Market) by the Gospel Music Association. **KAVX** (Today's Teaching and Talk: A Voice to Christ) went on the air in 1998. It was the 2004 Station of the Year (Talk Format).

Dwyan is a graduate of Texas Tech University and Christ for the Nations Institute. He was ordained in 1977 and is the pastor of Calvary Chapel in Lufkin, Texas.

The best advice I ever got ...

Genuine friendship requires time, trust, and vulnerability.

At a time when I was terribly concerned about my business, my good friend Robert said to me, "I don't have any answers, but if the worst comes to pass, whatever I have is yours."

We had been friends for a dozen years and really clicked. Our mutual interest in business was a factor, but our personalities meshed too. So it was natural for me to share my business problems when they became bigger than my own ingenuity.

But Robert's response floored me. Of course, I could never take him up on his offer, but his act of true friendship reminded me of the God who owns the cattle on a thousand hills. Suddenly the problems seemed minuscule. I knew God would provide for me. By being my friend, Robert had shown me how much God loved me, and I knew I would be all right.

To succeed past the cliché level of friendship requires an investment of time, trust, and vulnerability. But the reward will be a genuine friend. True friendship, just like anything else worthwhile, requires work. No amount of money or prestige will ever compare to the friendships that have developed in my life. This, to me, is one of the measures of true success.

Patrick Morley

Entrepreneur, Author, and Speaker

Jesus said, "My command is this:
Love each other as I have loved you.
Greater love has no one than this,
that he lay down his life for his friends."

John 15:12–13

Two are better than one,
    because they have a good return for their work:
If one falls down,
    his friend can help him up.
But pity the man who falls
    and has no one to help him up!...
Though one may be overpowered,
    two can defend themselves.
A cord of three strands is not quickly broken.

Ecclesiastes 4:9–10, 12

Since the late 1980s, Patrick Morley has been one of America's most respected authorities on the unique challenges facing men. In 1973, he founded Morley Properties, which was hailed as one of Florida's one hundred largest privately held companies. He was also the president or managing partner of fifty-nine companies and partnerships.

In 1989, Patrick Morley wrote the bestselling book, *The Man in the Mirror*, which poured from his own search for meaning and a deeper relationship with God. In 1991, he sold his business and founded Man in the Mirror, a ministry which "exists in answer to the prayers of all those wives, mothers, and grandmothers who have for decades been praying for the men in their lives."

Man in the Mirror's faculty members conduct church sponsored men's events nationwide to reach every man in America with a credible offer of salvation and the resources to grow in Christ. He also chairs the Steering Committee for the National Coalition of Men's Ministries.

The best advice I ever got ...

Destroy sexual temptation with prayer.

As I was growing in my Christian life and ministry, I heard a highly respected woman minister give this advice. She told of an incident when she found herself suddenly attracted to a fellow minister she had been serving with for years. When their eyes met, she realized that he felt it too. Sensing that this was an effort by the enemy to destroy their service to God and others, she went to her room and knelt in prayer, staying on her knees until she sensed the temptation had passed.

The intimacy formed when praying and counseling with others can be fertile ground for sexual temptation. This is why so many ministers enter into inappropriate, sinful relationships that destroy families and cost them their ministries. Attacking the emotions with logic, depending upon one's own willpower, or discussing the situation with the other person involved can easily backfire; but quickly running to God and staying in his presence until the temptation has passed is the surest way to keep one's heart and thoughts pure.

This advice has helped me keep my ministry untarnished through the years, and I'm pleased to be able to offer it to future generations.

Sue Parks
Teacher and Minister

Jesus said, "Watch and pray so that you will not fall into temptation. The spirit is willing, but the body is weak."

Matthew 26:41

Shun youthful lusts and flee from them, and aim at and pursue righteousness (all that is virtuous and good, right living, conformity to the will of God in thought, word, and deed); [and aim at and pursue] faith, love, [and] peace (harmony and concord with others) in fellowship with all [Christians], who call upon the Lord out of a pure heart.

2 Timothy 2:22 AMP

Submit yourselves, then, to God. Resist the devil, and he will flee from you. Come near to God and he will come near to you.

James 4:7–8

Sue Parks has led a rich and fruitful life as a result of God's grace and her willingness to serve.

In the 1950s, she served as a dedicated schoolteacher. In the 1960s, she helped many young adults grow closer to God by opening her home and teaching them the Bible, praying for them, nurturing them, and helping them grow in their spiritual walk.

Later, Sue and her husband, Courtney, served as Christian camp directors, and she was ordained as a minister by Trinity Christian Church in Houston, Texas, in 1977. In the 1980s, Sue received a master's degree in counseling and pastoral care from Houston Graduate School of Theology.

In the 1990s, she helped to establish an outstanding hospital chaplaincy program; and for five years, she served as the pastor of Broadmoor Christian Church in Houston.

Now, at age eighty, she continues to serve as a teacher, counselor, and minister to all those who need her.

The best advice I ever got ...

Read the book of Proverbs.

Although I had been encouraged to read the Bible throughout my early Sunday school years, it was during my "turbulent teens" that I received the advice to read this specific book. A couple of counselors at a basketball camp I attended suggested this after I disclosed a desire to change the way I was thinking and acting around my friends, peers, and family. I had been heading down a dangerous path during this time in my life and I wanted to change my behavior, but I knew it was going to take more than just willpower. The counselors told me that Proverbs was filled with good advice on how to live a joyful and meaningful life. That sure sounded good to me, so I did it.

Seeking wisdom through the book of Proverbs helped me in several ways. First, it was easy for me to read and understand, so I began using God's Word as a practical guide for my life. Second, Proverbs is filled with rich advice on how to live. It became apparent to me that I was *not* living as God wanted, and this led me to make some serious changes in my personal behavior choices. Finally, this led me to honestly seek wisdom and understanding, which ultimately led me to make the life-changing decision to receive Jesus Christ as my Lord and Savior.

Kelly Baughman

Associate Pastor, Chaplain, Teacher, and Musician

Accept my words.
Store up my commands inside you.
Let your ears listen to wisdom.
Apply your heart to understanding.
Call out for the ability to be wise.
Cry out for understanding.
Look for it as you would look for silver.
Search for it as you would search for hidden
        treasure. . . .
You will understand what is right and honest and fair.
You will understand the right way to live.
Your heart will become wise.
Your mind will delight in knowledge.
Good sense will keep you safe.

Proverbs 2:1–4, 9–11 NIrV

Kelly Baughman is proof positive that God can bring good out of tragic circumstances. In 1994, Kelly and his wife, Kathy, lost their seven-year-old daughter to a rare immune deficiency, following a two-year battle and numerous hospital stays. During this time, Kelly developed a passion for the sick and lonely as well as their caregivers and created a course entitled *Balance before Burnout* to encourage and educate those serving in high-stress care-giving capacities. He later taught this course as an adjunct faculty member for Seattle Pacific University.

Since 1979, Kelly has taught every grade from kindergarten through middle school. He has been a high-school girls' basketball coach and was named Coach of the Year for their league in 1986. For the last twelve years, he has served in numerous retirement and nursing homes, hospitals, and rehab centers. He presently serves as a healthcare chaplain with Healthcare Chaplains Ministry Association and calls himself "The Singin' Chaplain," at Children's Hospital in Seattle. Since 2004, he has been the associate pastor over pastoral care and church assimilation at Mountain View Community Church of Snohomish, Washington.

The best advice I ever got ...

Focus on your big dream!

I received this simple but profound advice from one of my high school football coaches, Larry Facchine. A very passionate competitor, Coach Facchine continually instilled in us what it meant to be a winner — how winners thought, what winners did. Not only did he encourage us to dream big, he also taught us how to fight through and overcome the obstacles we faced in order to become successful.

One of the most effective exercises he taught us took place in the locker room before each game. After turning off the lights, he would tell us to relax and focus on what we were about to do on the field. We were then to visualize a successful outcome. That season our team was undefeated and won the championship in Western Pennsylvania. We achieved our dream.

Coach Facchine showed us how to take *focus* to the next level. That lesson enabled me to achieve success in professional football. Later I realized that I could apply the same principles to my spiritual walk. As I began to focus on God and seek him with all my heart, I developed a passion for those things God cares about. That's real success.

Steve August
Athlete, Business Owner, and Speaker

"I know the plans I have for you," announces the Lᴏʀᴅ. "I want you to enjoy success. I do not plan to harm you. I will give you hope for the years to come. Then you will call out to me. You will come and pray to me. And I will listen to you. When you look for me with all your heart, you will find me."

Jeremiah 29:11–13 NIrV

May [the Lᴏʀᴅ] give you the desire of your heart and make all your plans succeed.

Psalm 20:4

Be all the more eager to make your calling and election sure. For if you do these things, you will never fall, and you will receive a rich welcome into the eternal kingdom of our Lord and Savior Jesus Christ.

2 Peter 1:10–11

Steve August's life as an athlete took off when he received a football scholarship to the University of Tulsa (Oklahoma) in the early 1970s. The offensive tackle was chosen as an all-conference player, and in 1976, he made the Missouri Valley Conference first team and was selected for the Associate Press Third-Team All-America. In the first round of the 1977 NFL draft, August was selected by the Seattle Seahawks, where he played for seven years and became an All-Pro. He was then traded to the Pittsburgh Steelers and later to the New York Jets. Due to injuries, August left the NFL after the 1985 season. He is a member of the Seahawks all-time team.

After coaching and teaching for three years in Seattle, Steve returned to Tulsa, where he earned a master's degree in sports management, with the goal of becoming an athletic director. However, after Steve married and his first son was born, he realized that a job requiring extensive travel and time away from home wasn't for him. It was then that he became a Certified Financial Planner. As vice president and part owner of Vineyard Financial Group, he is also certified by the Christian Financial Professionals Network. Steve speaks to various groups through the Fellowship of Christian Athletes and Stonecroft Ministries.

The best advice I ever got ...

Quit talking

and do it.

As an eighteen-year-old freshman, I tried out for the varsity lacrosse team at Cornell University, one of the top ten programs in the country. I hadn't been playing well and went into the coach's office and began rambling to him that he would see me playing better soon. As I continued to ramble, he cut me off in midsentence and stated bluntly, "Hey, kid, we play it." Then he literally kicked me out the door and said, "Now do it on the field." I got the message — quit talking and do it!

I was angry, but soon his words motivated me to practice more and play harder. Eventually I became one of only four freshmen to make the varsity travel squad. I realize now that he taught me the greatest lesson of all. Talkers talk and doers do. We speak loudest through our actions.

To this day, when I think about making a difference in the world, I remember my coach's words and ask myself, *What am I going to do today to serve, inspire, and help people?* Action is required. Saint Francis of Assisi said, "It's no use walking anywhere to preach unless your preaching is your walking." So every day I take a walk on the field of life and let my walking do my talking.

Jon Gordon

Speaker, Consultant, and Author

Dear children, let us not love with words or tongue but with actions and in truth.

1 John 3:18

Do not merely listen to the word, and so deceive yourselves. Do what it says.

James 1:22

Faith by itself, if it is not accompanied by action, is dead.... A person is justified by what he does and not by faith alone.

James 2:17, 24

The people who know their God will display strength and take action.

Daniel 11:32 NASB

Jon Gordon, known as "America's #1 Energy Coach," is a pioneer in the field of energy coaching — an integrative approach that blends positive psychology, emotional intelligence, nutrition, exercise, and bio-energy fields to enhance health, happiness, professional success, and athletic performance.

He is the bestselling author of *Energy Addict: 101 Mental, Physical, and Spiritual Ways to Energize Your Life* and *The 10-Minute Energy Solution.* He is also the co-founder of the **Positive Energy Program,** a nonprofit initiative to help develop healthy, positive kids.

As a professional speaker, Jon has infused energy into organizations such as **The PGA** Tour, **The Jacksonville Jaguars, Wachovia Bank, Chubb Insurance, Cingular Wireless, General Electric, State Farm Insurance, The United Way,** and the **Super Bowl Host Committee.** He and his energy tips have been featured on **N**AB 's *Today* and **CNN's** *American Morning* and in publications such as *WebMD, Men's Health, Self, Energy Times, Woman's Day,* **and** *Redbook.*

The best advice I ever got ...

Spend time with your children and don't work too much.

As a middle manager at a fairly sizable company, I found myself in a meeting one day with one of the most influential and senior executives. Before we started talking about the issue at hand, he asked if I had children. After I explained that I didn't yet, he said, "When you do, spend time with them and don't work too much. My son is eighteen, and I don't really know him." I was stunned.

A few years later, I started my own company and began to experience success and the demands that go with it. I quickly learned that the tendency to make work a higher priority than family — and faith — is a gradual, subtle, insidious process. I knew I would have to take overt, even painful steps to ensure that I would not be an executive in my fifties warning someone else not to fall into the workaholic trap.

Today I coach multiple junior sports teams, limit my travel to a handful of days each month, volunteer in our church and school, and eat breakfast and dinner with my wife and children on most days. I thank God for that humble, gracious man who took the time to share his painful wisdom with me.

Patrick Lencioni

Author, Speaker, and Consultant

Children are a heritage from the Lord,
  offspring a reward from him.
Like arrows in the hands of a warrior
  are children born in one's youth.
Blessed is the man
  whose quiver is full of them.
  Psalm 127:3–5 TNIV

Train children in the right way,
  and when old, they will not stray.
  Proverbs 22:6 NRSV

In the fear of the Lord one has strong confidence,
  and one's children will have a refuge.
  Proverbs 14:26 NRSV

Patrick Lencioni is the founder and president of The Table Group, Inc., a specialized management-consulting firm focused on organizational health. Since establishing the firm in 1997, Pat has become one of the nation's leading experts on executive team development.

Pat's passion for organizations and teams is reflected in his writing, speaking, and consulting. He is the author of four business books including *The Five Dysfunctions of a Team*, which continues to be highlighted on *The New York Times*, *BusinessWeek*, *Wall Street Journal*, and *USA Today* bestseller lists. His earlier successes include *Death by Meeting*, *The Four Obsessions of an Extraordinary Executive*, and *The Five Temptations of a CEO*. Pat's work has been featured in numerous publications such as *Fast Company*, *INC Magazine*, *USA Today*, *Entrepreneur*, and *The Harvard Business Review*.

Prior to founding The Table Group, Pat worked at Bain & Company, Oracle Corporation and Sybase, where he was vice president of organizational development. He also served on the national board of directors for the Make-A-Wish Foundation of America from 2000–2003.

The best advice I ever got ...

What would you do with the rest of your life if you weren't afraid?

Years ago, a pastor and friend of mine asked this question during a sermon. My first thought was, *What do you mean by that? I'm not afraid!* But as I thought about it, I began to see what he was really saying.

Whenever I begin to lose my courage and step back from a particular person or project, I ask myself, *What would you do now if you weren't afraid?* It could be a fear of failing, fear that there won't be enough money to pay the bills, fear that important people will walk away at a critical time, fear that God won't come through on this one, or fear that I really didn't hear his voice to begin with.

Fear, doubt, and unbelief hang around each of us, waiting to snatch unique opportunities out of our hands. They seek to cripple us into a state of inaction.

We write books about those who overcome these paralyzing fears and press on to win the prize. The truth is, God has given all of us the tools we need to succeed at his plan for our lives. If he is for us, who — or what — can be against us?

Paul Wilbur

Recording Artist

"Do not fear, for I am with you;
    do not be dismayed, for I am your God.
I will strengthen you and help you;
    I will uphold you with my righteous right hand,"
says the LORD.
        Isaiah 41:10

If God is for us, who can be against us? He who did not spare his
own Son, but gave him up for us all — how will he not also, along
with him, graciously give us all things?
        Romans 8:31–32

The LORD said, "Be strong and courageous.
Do not be terrified; do not be discouraged, for the LORD
your God will be with you wherever you go."
        Joshua 1:9

In God I trust; I will not be afraid.
What can man do to me?
        Psalm 56:11

Paul Wilbur is an Integrity Music recording artist and the founder of Wilbur Ministries. He and his team travel throughout the United States and the world sharing the love of God through Yeshua (Jesus) the Messiah.

In 1990, Paul recorded his first release with Integrity entitled *Up to Zion*. Since then he has recorded four more solo albums, including three performed live in Jerusalem — *Shalom Jerusalem*, *Lion of Judah*, and *Jerusalem Arise!* — all of which have become favorites around the world.

Paul has also recorded six projects in Spanish and two in Portuguese, and is currently in the process of recording *Shalom Jerusalem* in Russian. These albums in different translations enable the team to minister to more than half of the world's population in their own language.

The best advice I ever got ...

Life is unpredictable.
Always have a backup plan.

My parents deserve the credit for instilling this principle in me. From doing household chores, to babysitting, to working as an educator, and even when planning parties, I was always encouraged to have a primary plan as well as a backup plan, in case things didn't go as expected.

Because I spend my day with children, I always plan for the unexpected. Because they are introduced to many new things and are faced with daily challenges as they grow, children are very unpredictable. I try to remain flexible and have my backup plan ready to implement when needed. My goal is to ensure that each child's day flows smoothly and that we stay as close as possible to a familiar routine. Providing security and balance in the classroom helps the children feel nurtured so that they can be open to learn.

I also benefit from the security that planning and executing a routine provides. At the same time, having knowledge of alternatives is comforting and allows me to grow. My parents' advice has proven to be invaluable, and I attribute much of my success to it.

Lynda Wingo

School Owner and Administrator

Be prepared in season and out of season.
2 Timothy 4:2

Commit to the LORD whatever you do,
and your plans will succeed.
Proverbs 16:3

Plan carefully and you will have plenty; if you act too quickly, you
will never have enough.
Proverbs 21:5 GNT

Do your best to present yourself to God as one approved, a worker
who does not need to be ashamed.
2 Timothy 2:15 TNIV

Having spent the last thirty-three years in various aspects of education, **Lynda Wingo** is the executive director and owner of Miss Helen's Private School, a learning institution specializing in early childhood education for preschoolers, kindergartners, and children in the first through fifth grades. Founded in 1954 by Lynda's mother-in-law, Helen Wingo, Miss Helen's is still family owned and operated. Lynda has been with the school since 1974.

Lynda is also committed to the growth and well-being of her community. She is an avid volunteer and fund-raiser for the Chamber of Commerce and other community-based and business-oriented organizations.

The best advice I ever got ...

You must be willing
to walk down
the street naked.

After six years as a missionary in Africa and during my third year as a pastor in Atlanta, I decided to write for publication. In the 1970s, I started a small group called the Scribe Tribe and we tried to teach each other to write. After a couple of years, professional writer Charlotte Hale joined us. At one meeting, she looked over something I had written, paused, and stared into my eyes. "This is all right, but if you are going to write, you must be willing to walk down the street naked."

I knew what she meant: I needed to become vulnerable. Instead, I had hidden my true feelings behind the words I had written.

Too often, writers and speakers say the right words — or the words they think people want to hear. I've learned that when I'm open and defenseless, people respect me and my position, even if they don't agree. Sensing that I have nothing to hide, they drop their defenses.

I often say about myself: I would rather be disliked for who I am than to be respected for who I am not.

Cecil "Cec" Murphey
Writer and Former Missionary

The apostle Paul wrote, "We have spoken freely to you, Corinthians, and opened wide our hearts to you."
2 Corinthians 6:11

"Go to the people I send you to, and tell them everything I command you to say. Do not be afraid of them, for I will be with you to protect you. I, the Lord, have spoken!" Then the Lord reached out, touched my lips, and said to me, "Listen, I am giving you the words you must speak."
Jeremiah 1:7–9 GNT

Kings take pleasure in honest lips;
they value a man who speaks the truth.
Proverbs 16:13

Cecil ("Cec") Murphey is a former missionary to Kenya and was a pastor for fourteen years. He has written, co-written, or ghostwritten more than one hundred books, both fiction and nonfiction. His best-known works are *90 Minutes in Heaven* (written for **Don Piper**); *Gifted Hands* (written for **Dr. Ben Carson**); and *Rebel with a Cause* (written for **Franklin Graham**). His books have been condensed in *Reader's Digest*, and **Disney is producing a film called** *The Mighty Bishops*, **based on his book** *I Choose to Stay* (written for **Salome Thomas-EL**). In addition, **Cecil has written theological books as well as a series for caregivers and books on Christian living. The articles he has written number more than six hundred.**

Murphey is the only writer to win the Dixie Council of Authors and Journalists award three times. In addition, he has won the Silver Angel award for excellence in print media and the Gold Medallion award. He holds master's degrees in theology and education.

The best advice I ever got ...

Four keys to getting through "Goliath" problems:

1. No problem can beat you unless you let it (Joseph, Genesis 37–50).

2. In every problem there is an opportunity, if you can look into the eye of the storm (Ezekiel 1).

3. God has a great law of recovery. Christians are like super balls — when compressed, they store up energy to bounce back even higher than before (Job).

4. No matter what happens, our Father owns the company. (The Rockefeller sons were sent to work in the hot dusty oil fields of Oklahoma.)

I drew this advice from a sermon by Pastor Richard Dresselhouse. The truth of it struck me so hard that I wrote down the four main points and illustrations and put them into my wallet. Eventually I created a card with these truths on it and occasionally passed it out to friends or patients going through major problems.

Whether we attempt to do something of significance or are just living life, we all encounter Goliath-sized problems. In my own life when this has happened, I get out my card, review the examples, then pray and look for the way *through* the problem. It is always there.

When my colleagues and I were starting the first Christian family medicine residency program, we often felt intimidated by Goliath-sized problems. We faced even more when we were starting our overseas conference and consultation model for medical missions. And when we started our mobile medical ministry for the underserved by partnering with churches, we faced even more seemingly insurmountable problems. But by applying the principles I learned from Pastor Dresselhouse and with God's help, we have been able to pioneer these ministries and meet the needs of people.

Dr. John Crouch

Physician and Medical Missionary

hope. Others make us suffer. But God does not desert us. We are knocked down. But we are not knocked out.

2 Corinthians 4:8–9 NIrV

Give thanks to God! He always leads us in the winners' parade because we belong to Christ.

2 Corinthians 2:14 NIrV

[The Lord] stilled the storm to a whisper;
the waves of the sea were hushed.
They were glad when it grew calm,
and he guided them to their desired haven.

Psalm 107:29–30

The Lord said, "Those who hope in me will not be disappointed."

Isaiah 49:23

Dr. John Crouch's career began with a tour as a medical officer and battalion flight surgeon for the U.S. Army in Vietnam where he earned the Air Medal and the Bronze Star. From there, he went on to practice emergency medicine and family practice in San Bernardino, California, and held various positions of instruction and administration. He joined the staff of Oral Roberts University School of Medicine in 1978.

In 1990, he helped form Family Medical Care of Tulsa and In His Image Family Medicine Residency Program. Through In His Image International, Dr. Crouch's vision has been to train residents for short-term mission trips and encourage long-term overseas service for full-time missionaries. He continues to help establish residency programs overseas.

In addition, Dr. Crouch helped co-found Good Samaritan Health Services, Inc., a mobile outreach providing accessible, affordable, whole-person care for the underserved.

You will catch more
flies with sugar
than with vinegar.

My mother was a wise woman. She carefully taught me how to deal with people — especially the difficult ones. "You will find that more people will pay attention to your opinion if you present it in a non-confrontational manner. When you come on strong, people often become defensive and the relationship becomes adversarial. But when you let other people know by your words and body language that you respect them, they will almost always respond favorably," she often reminded me.

My mom also taught me that there is something nice you can say about every person. Focusing on that one good thing will give you a clear advantage.

This does not mean that we should be two-faced and superficial. But it does mean that *how* you say something is as important as *what* you say. Those who can take hold of that truth and incorporate it into their lives will be much more successful in everything they try.

Roberta Shaffer

Minister

One who loves a pure heart and who speaks with grace
will have the king for a friend.
Proverbs 22:11 TNIV

Your speech should always be pleasant and interesting, and you
should know how to give the right answer to everyone.
Colossians 4:6 GNT

A gentle answer quiets anger,
but a harsh one stirs it up. Kind words bring life.
Proverbs 15:1, 4 GNT

Kind words are like honey — sweet
to the taste and good for your health.
Proverbs 16:24 GNT

When we are insulted, we answer back with kind words.
1 Corinthians 4:13 GNT

Do not use harmful words, but only helpful words, the
kind that build up and provide what is needed, so that
what you say will do good to those who hear you.
Ephesians 4:29 GNT

Roberta Shaffer's call to ministry came while at high school church camp. Since she had never met a woman in ministry except a missionary, she was sure God must have been speaking to the boy standing next to her! After twenty-five years of lay ministry as a teacher, youth leader, Christian education director, and contemporary worship leader, Shaffer received a Master of Divinity from Phillips Theological Seminary in Tulsa, OK. She currently serves a Disciples of Christ & Church of Brethren congregation, Woodgrove Parish, in Hastings, Michigan.

The best advice I ever got ...

No one can be everything to another person.

When my daughter was born, I felt a huge amount of responsibility to be sure that I was able to give her everything she needed. I often felt discouraged and anxious sensing that I was unable to ensure her future success or even keep her as safe and well as I thought I should.

Once, while I was murmuring and self-deprecating to a woman at my church, she interrupted and simply said to me: "You can't be everything to your daughter or to anyone else. Pray that God will bridge the gap between what you can give her and what she needs." Those words were a revelation and a relief to me.

I've incorporated that principle into every area of my life. Before I begin a writing project, prepare for a speaking engagement, or deal with an issue with a friend or family member, I pray that God will bridge the gap between what I can give and what is needed.

This does not mean that I ever do less than my very best, but it does allow me to accept my limitations and refocus my perspective onto God's vast resources. What I really love is when I realize that God is using me to bridge the gap for someone else.

Nancy Rue

Author and Speaker

My God will liberally supply (fill to the full) your every need
according to His riches in glory in Christ Jesus.

Philippians 4:19 AMP

I commend you to the care of God and to the message
of his grace, which is able to build you up and give you
the blessings God has for all his people.

Acts 20:32 GNT

We have not stopped praying for you and asking God to fill you
with the knowledge of his will ... that you may live a life worthy of
the Lord and may please him in every way: bearing fruit in every
good work, growing in the knowledge of God.

Colossians 1:9–10

I pray that out of his glorious riches he may strengthen
you with power through his Spirit in your inner being,
so that Christ may dwell in your hearts through faith ...
that you, being rooted and established in love, may have
power ... to grasp how wide and long and high and deep
is the love of Christ, and to know this love that surpasses
knowledge—that you may be filled to the measure of all the
fullness of God.

Ephesians 3:16–19

The Mystery of Eleanor Village was **Nancy Rue's** first novel . . . attempt. After cranking out three chapters on a manual typewriter and presenting them for parental review ("It moves a little fast, doesn't it?" was the verdict), into the trash it went, along with her writing career, until she found herself teaching a high school writing course and trying to make sense of the poor writing textbook. In an effort to do a better job for her students, she started completing all the assignments with them. The pieces fell into place and now her readers can't get enough of her writing.

Nancy centers her ministry around our need to be the authentic selves God created us to be. To that end, she has written over eighty books for tweens, teens, and women, including the fabulous *Lily* series for Zondervan. She also speaks and teaches extensively.

The best advice I ever got ...

You can change the pictures of your life's story.

In high school, the pictures of my life story were a mess. I grew up in a single-parent home and struggled with anger and a deep fear of loss and rejection. Then I started attending Young Life meetings and met Doug Barram, an ex-football player with a huge heart for kids and love for Christ. After a year of listening to Doug's talks, I asked Jesus into my heart — and that same night I received some of the best advice I've ever heard.

Handing me my first Bible, Doug turned to Hebrews 13:5b and told me to read those few words *"one hundred times."* He *meant* to read them *several* times, but I took his words literally. One hundred times, a lonely, fearful, angry young man read: "[Jesus] Himself has said, I will never leave you nor forsake you" **(NASV)**. With my background, going away to college brought lots of anxiety. The anxiety disappeared that night.

I left for college with the incredible security that Jesus would always be with me and never leave nor forsake me. The pictures of my life's story had once been lonely and dismal, but Doug's advice and God's Word teamed up to change all that. They can give you the power to change the pictures of your life story as well.

John Trent

Physician, Teacher, Speaker, and Author

[You] have put on the new self, which is being renewed in

knowledge in the image of its Creator.
Colossians 3:10

As he thinketh in his heart, so is he.
Proverbs 23:7 KJV

Don't live any longer the way this world lives. Let your way of thinking be completely changed. Then you will be able to test what God wants for you. And you will agree that what he wants is right. His plan is good and pleasing and perfect.
Romans 12:2 NIrV

Always think about what is true. Think about what is noble, right and pure. Think about what is lovely and worthy of respect. If anything is excellent or worthy of praise, think about those kinds of things.
Philippians 4:8 NIrV

John Trent is president and founder of StrongFamilies.com, an outreach committed to strengthening relationships worldwide. Through their website (www.strongfamilies.com) his goal is to sign up *one million families* to become, "**Homes of Light**" — strong families who get relationship help and hope — and then reach out to another family in their neighborhood or extended family.

Trent teaches at numerous conferences across the country and has authored and co-authored more than a dozen award-winning and bestselling books. He has also written six books for children.

In addition to Trent's speaking at marriage and family conferences across the country, he has spoken extensively to corporate America. In these sessions, Trent shares principles that help strengthen employees' relationships with their families and with each other. For example, Trent has created an online assessment called, Workplace Insights, that only takes ten minutes to complete online, then instantly emails back a 28-page strengths assessment. Using humor, powerful graphics, and quickly grasped relationship tools, Trent has helped numerous companies realize that strong families are a key to building strong companies.

The best advice I ever got ...

Author Index

Plans fail for lack of counsel,
But with many advisers they succeed.
Proverbs 15:22

Notes

Notes

At Inspirio, we would love to hear your

stories and your feedback.

Please send your comments to us

by way of email at

icares@zondervan.com

or to the address below:

inspirio

Attn: Inspirio Cares

5300 Patterson Avenue SE

Grand Rapids, MI 49530

If you would like further information

about Inspirio and the products we

create, please visit us at:

www.inspiriogifts.com

Thank you and God bless!